WOMEN AT THE WELL

*32 Refreshing Devotions
for a Thirsty Soul*

❊ ❊ ❊

COMPILED BY BETTY ROBISON

TYNDALE HOUSE PUBLISHERS INC., WHEATON, ILLINOIS

Visit Tyndale's exciting Web site at www.tyndale.com

Women at the Well: 32 Refreshing Devotions for a Thirsty Soul

Copyright © 2003 by Betty Robison. All rights reserved.

Cover illustration by Timothy Thompson. All rights reserved.

Author photograph by Feragne Photography copyright © 2003 by Life Outreach International. All rights reserved.

Designed by Beth Sparkman

Edited by Ramona Cramer Tucker and Susan Taylor

We gratefully acknowledge the publishers and authors from which some of the enclosed material has been adapted (see sources).

Unless otherwise indicated, all Scripture quotations are taken from the *Holy Bible*, New Living Translation, copyright © 1996. Used by permission of Tyndale House Publishers, Inc., Wheaton, Illinois 60189. All rights reserved.

Scripture quotations marked NIV are taken from the *Holy Bible*, New International Version®. NIV®. Copyright © 1973, 1978, 1984 by International Bible Society. Used by permission of Zondervan Publishing House. All rights reserved.

Scripture quotations marked "NKJV" are taken from the New King James Version. Copyright © 1979, 1980, 1982, 1991 by Thomas Nelson, Inc. Used by permission. All rights reserved.

Scripture verses marked Phillips are taken from *The New Testament in Modern English* by J. B. Phillips, copyright © J. B. Phillips, 1958, 1959, 1960, 1972. All rights reserved.

Scripture quotations marked GNT are taken from the Good News Translation in Today's English Version–Second Edition copyright © 1992 by American Bible Society. Used by permission.

Library of Congress Cataloging-in-Publication Data

Printed in the United States of America

09 08 07 06 05 04 03
7   6   5   4   3   2   1

CONTENTS

PART THREE: SPIRIT

Introduction

I love to rise early and have my quiet, secluded time with the Lord. It gives me the opportunity to pause and listen to what he wants to say to me as I place before him all my needs and burdens for others in prayer. By doing so every day, I find fulfillment in my whole being and feel better prepared to meet the challenges of my day.

Those "quiet times" with the Lord are like living water that flows over me. I love the way the New Living Translation interprets Colossians 2:6-7: "And now, just as you accepted Christ Jesus as your Lord, you must continue to live in obedience to him. Let your roots grow down into him and draw up nourishment from him, so you will grow in faith, strong and vigorous in the truth you were taught. Let your lives overflow with thanksgiving for all he has done."

As I let my "roots grow down into him," my mind is renewed. I begin to see his perspective, rather than my own finite one, and I also begin to interact in my other relationships with more love, joy, peace, patience, kindness, goodness, faithfulness, gentleness, and self-control (see Galatians 5:22-23) than I could have on my own power. I become energized by the Holy Spirit, and the very character and nature of Christ begin to grow and be evidenced in my life . . . no matter the circumstances under which I find myself at the time.

The idea for *Women at the Well* was derived from my own experiences of spiritual growth and my longing to inspire others who are in varied life circumstances. Thus, this devotional addresses the "hot issues"—such as infertility, loneliness, depression, body image, and abortion—as well as a woman's daily challenges (developing confidence, cultivating contentment, dealing with change, comparing herself to others physically, emotionally, and spiritually). It contains personal insights from more than twenty-five other women too, who, just like you and me, juggle myriad roles throughout their days. Each "day" includes a short devotional, "Words of Life" from the Scriptures, a personal challenge through "Living It Out," and then a concluding "Drawing from the Well of Prayer."

Inside *Women at the Well*, you'll find three distinct parts because I believe God created us with three aspects of our beings: *soul, body,* and *spirit.* The *soul* is our individual and essential being. It has three basic functions: the mind, the will, and the emotions. The *body* is our physical housing of our soul and spirit. The *spirit* is our invisible nature or what we truly are. What is so amazing is that God so intricately interwove these three aspects of a woman's life that *all* are affected if one is out of balance.

And it's so easy to get out of balance. After all, it's Satan's driving ambition to disconnect our lifelines to Jesus. He has many deceptive devices, and if we allow him to get his foot in the door of our lives, we can quickly become his victims. His oppression and darkness can sweep over our souls, our spirits, and even our bodies.

But the apostle Paul's letter to the Colossian Christians offers us valuable insight into guarding against Satan's deception: "Don't let anyone lead you astray with empty philosophy and high-sounding nonsense that come from human thinking and from the evil powers of this world, and not from Christ. For in Christ the fullness of God lives in a human body, and you are complete through your union with Christ. He is the Lord over every ruler and authority in the universe" (Colossians 2:8-10).

Through some difficult life experiences and through studying Scripture, I am continually learning how to be alert and recognize Satan's deceptions. That awareness has given me a passionate sense of responsibility to keep the pathway cleared in all three areas—to be complete and strive for Christlikeness in my soul, spirit, *and* body.

I've also learned how vital good communication is—whether in relationships with your family and loved ones that go beyond the surface or in growing a deeper fellowship with the Lord. Drawing from the well of the Lord's wisdom and love takes time, but it's well worth it.

Every day I discover more about how our fellowship can take on a new dimension when we commit our lives and submit our wills to Christ (see Romans 12:1-2). We must seek to learn from him, his life, and his teachings. We must recognize and ask for the Holy Spirit's fullness and power—not just in times of crisis, but *daily*. That's why my prayer for you is that this devotional will not only encourage you by addressing the felt needs in your life but also help you to set aside a special time of intimate communication between you and the Lord.

For it is only in total dependence and in vital union with the Lord that we'll have everything we need in our soul, body, and spirit for each day. And it's only when we recognize his power that we will truly be thankful for each moment he gives us to serve him. May you be filled to overflowing as you draw from *Women at the Well*, and may you experience more fully the power and love of a living God who cares about every area of your life.

Betty Robison

Part One

SOUL

Betty Robison

Betty Robison cohosts the
LIFE TODAY television show
with her husband, James.
She is the mother of three children
and the grandmother of eleven.
She and James have been
married for forty years
and live in the
Dallas–Fort Worth area.

Waiting for God's Best

Our first child, Rhonda, was three years old when I had an ovary removed. The doctor said I had endometriosis and advised me to focus on enjoying my daughter because I probably wouldn't be able to conceive any more children. My heart sank. I longed to have a son. I cried out to God with the prayer of Hannah in 1 Samuel 1:11: "O Lord Almighty . . . look down upon my sorrow and answer my prayer and give me a son." When my miracle didn't come, I grew jealous of other women who were able to have babies, and worse yet, I became bitter and angry at God.

One day in my brokenness over this spiritual impasse, I finally released my hurt and anger to God. I asked him to heal me of the profound disappointment of not being able to have another child. I asked him to fill the empty space inside me. With tears streaming down my face, I told him, "I just want to live for you. I want to relish every moment you've given me to spend with my precious Rhonda."

In time God graciously began to take away the yearning I had to give birth to a son. And, amazingly, he filled my heart with a peace and contentment I had previously thought was impossible. With the contentment came a peaceful desire to check into adoption. A lawyer friend helped my husband, James, and me apply to several agencies. After our first meeting with him, he started the paperwork, and the wait began. Providentially, exactly nine months from the date of that meeting, our son, James Randall, came into the world and into our hearts forever.

The first time James and I saw Randy, our eyes filled with tears of pure joy. We kept saying, "He's so beautiful. I can't believe he's ours!" We loved him from that first moment

BETTY ROBISON

and have never stopped since! There was no difference in the intensity of our love for our adopted son and our love for our biological daughter.

Over three years later I began to feel unusually tired and a little queasy. I was concerned that maybe the endometriosis was back in full force. I went to the doctor, thinking I had cancer. Instead, James and I found out that a miracle had occurred—I was pregnant! On November 18, 1972, Robin Rochelle Robison, our miracle baby, joined our family, making it complete.

As I tucked my three little Rs into bed one night and gave them good-night kisses, I reflected on God's perfect plan. He had wanted me to have his best. If he'd given me what I wanted, *when* I wanted it, I never would have known our wonderful son, Randy.

Since then, whenever my heart is hurting over a troubling situation, I strive to remember that God has a plan and he sees the whole picture. He knows *what* I need and *when* I need it. Although it can be hard to wait on him, I cling to the truth that he wants to bless me with *his* best in *his* perfect time.

Words of Life

The Lord God is our light and protector. He gives us grace and glory. No good thing will the Lord withhold from those who do what is right. O Lord Almighty, happy are those who trust in you. *Psalm 84:11-12* ❧ He gives the barren woman a home, so that she becomes a happy mother. Praise the Lord! *Psalm 113:9* ❧ There is a special rest still waiting for the people of God. For all who enter into God's rest will find rest from their labors, just as God rested after creating the world. Let us do our best to enter that place of rest. For anyone who disobeys God, as the people of Israel did, will fall. *Hebrews 4:9-11* ❧ I am sure that God, who began the good work within you, will continue his work until it is finally finished on that day when Christ Jesus comes back again. . . . For God is working in you, giving you the desire to obey him and the power to do what pleases him. *Philippians 1:6; 2:13*

LIVING IT OUT

Ephesians 2:10 says we were created for good works, the kind that are done through dependence on God. Remember that the work being done in your life is God's work and, therefore, will be done on his timetable. Rest in God's ability, and reap the supernatural results. Be careful not to rob yourself of joy, peace, and fulfillment *while he is working* by fretting over the time he's taking to get it done. Remember that God demonstrates his heart of sensitivity toward you by blessing you with his best in his time.

Drawing from the Well of Prayer

Oh, how I praise the Lord. How I rejoice in God my Savior! For he took notice of his lowly servant girl. . . . He, the Mighty One, is holy, and he has done great things for me.

Luke 1:46-49, from the prayer of Mary, the mother of Jesus, as she realized she indeed was pregnant with the Christ child

Bonnie Budzowski

Bonnie Budzowski, a freelance writer and communications consultant, lives in Pittsburgh, Pennsylvania. Her company, WordCoach, helps organizations to meet their challenges in written and oral communication. Bonnie, who holds an M.A. in communications and an M.A. in biblical studies, lives with her husband, Rick, and her adopted daughter, Meagan.

When Loneliness Strikes

When my friend Pauline's roommate moved away, Pauline couldn't find another, no matter how hard she tried. As she moved alone into a new apartment, she felt unattached, vulnerable, and afraid for her safety. Questions and doubts rumbled inside her: How would she handle living alone? Did she have what it takes to create an inviting home? Who would take care of her in years to come?

As we talked about her feelings of loneliness, Pauline was surprised to learn that intense loneliness strikes *all* women—not just single women. The experience can be mild or intense, the causes simple or complex. While Pauline and I can point to difficult circumstances as the cause of our loneliness (mine was my childlessness), others can't. Sometimes there's just a vague, empty feeling, like a cloud over the day.

How can we escape this loneliness? Society encourages us to entertain ourselves or acquire things. Well-meaning friends advise us to reject self-pity and get involved in the lives of others. Yet when we're exhausted from service to others, the voice of loneliness can still haunt us—and surface again and again over the years. Loneliness is simply a reality of living in a fallen world.

When Adam and Eve sinned, their relationship with God and with each other was broken, and loneliness was one of the results. Now all people, even those in the best of circumstances, experience separation from others and God. The death of a loved one, a divorce, a romantic breakup, a serious illness, a child's leaving home, a long-distance move—all can trigger overwhelming loneliness.

In such times, it helps to look at Jesus' example. Surely he understands how we feel.

He had no spouse, no children, no true peers. His earthly companionship consisted of a few friends and some scraggly followers who deserted him at his darkest hour. And on the cross, when the world's sin separated Jesus from his Father, his loneliness was so intense that he cried out, "My God, my God, why have you forsaken me?"

Yet just as Jesus learned obedience to the Father through the things he suffered, so must we. The solution to the problem of loneliness doesn't lie in increased activity but in facing the reality of our loneliness and seeking the presence of God within it.

After much struggle I began to accept loneliness as a natural part of life. I stopped frantically trying to fill my days and adopted an attitude of submission to God. I finally considered God's plans rather than my own and as a result, began to look beyond my infertility to explore other ways of having a child. Pauline, too, now looks for the most useful way to submit her current circumstances to God, although she still longs to be married one day.

When I took my pain to God in prayer, not for a way out but for comfort, the acute tension I felt began to subside. As I began to seek God more for himself than for the solutions he could provide, my relationship with him deepened and became more satisfying. I found relief from self-pity and a comfort in knowing that God really does have everything under control. No matter what happens, nothing can separate me from his love. And God's Word assures us that our suffering won't last forever. Romans 8:18-39 tells us that one day Christ will return and all creation will be redeemed. So while I long for the second coming of Christ, I cling to the promise of God's presence with me today. I may feel lonely, but I am never alone.

WORDS OF LIFE

O God, you are my God; I earnestly search for you. My soul thirsts for you; my whole body longs for you in this parched and weary land where there is no water. *Psalm 63:1* Can anything ever separate us from Christ's love? Does it mean he no longer loves us if we have trouble or calamity, or are persecuted, or are hungry or cold or in danger or threatened with death? . . . No, despite all these things, overwhelming victory is ours through Christ, who loved us. And I am convinced that nothing can ever separate us from his love. Death can't, and life can't. The angels can't, and the demons can't. Our fears for today, our worries about tomorrow, and even the powers of hell can't keep God's love away. Whether we are high above the sky or in the deepest ocean, nothing in all creation will ever be able to separate us from the love of God that is revealed in Christ Jesus our Lord. *Romans 8:35, 37-39*

LIVING IT OUT

Are you feeling lonely? If so, determine to live creatively and without bitterness, whatever the outcome. Ask God to give you an attitude of submission so you can move out of the self-pity trap into a place of peace and acceptance. Then look for ways in which you can extend this peace and comfort to others in similar situations. The options are endless, and the results can be encouraging to you, too, if instead of trying to escape your lonely moments, you ask God to work *through* them.

Drawing from the Well of Prayer

Lord, I admit it: I feel so lonely. I need others in my life, and I need a greater sense of your presence. Give me a hunger to know you more intimately. That's what I was created to do. Help me to work through my pain, to find solutions, and to deepen my relationship with you and with others.

Robin Turner

Robin Turner is the younger
daughter of James and Betty
Robison. She, her husband,
Ken, and their children live
in Tulsa, Oklahoma,
where Robin devotes herself
full-time to her ministry as
a wife and mother.

The Best Job in the World

When I was a young girl, people would ask me what I wanted to be when I grew up. As far back as I can remember, I would tell them I wanted to be a wife and mother. I even dressed up as a homemaker for career day in the ninth grade. I chose this as my career, and I think it's the most rewarding job there is.

But in spite of my strong maternal instincts, there are days when I feel as if I'm fighting a losing battle when it comes to training my children. Despite numerous, sometimes valiant efforts to correct undesirable behavior in my irresistible offspring, I find myself transformed into a parental Rocky—back in the ring and going the distance with a recurring problem.

Then something will happen to remind me that maybe all my effort and prayers are not in vain after all. One day when my children were small, I became very frustrated with them. My impatience grew by the minute and peaked when one of the boys dripped a trail of juice up the stairs. He *knew* he was supposed to keep his juice in the kitchen, but evidently my bad attitude had rubbed off on him . . . as well as the other children.

As I was putting folded laundry away, slamming the dresser drawers shut and grumbling under my breath, Christopher, one of my boys, looked at me with his big blue eyes and said, "Mom, you're not rejoicing in the Lord always!" Well, that woke me up! This was the same verse I had often quoted to the children, and now it was coming back to me—from the mouth of my babe.

I turned to Christopher and got down on my knees. "You're right, Son," I said. "Mommy needs to ask God's forgiveness, and I need to ask your forgiveness too."

Wrapping his sweet little arms around my neck, he gave me a tight squeeze. "That's okay, Mommy. I forgive you."

Then, by an act of my will, I chose to change my attitude and be joyful. As a result, I had a much better day, and my children became more joyful too.

Later that day I realized my young son had showed signs of spiritual sensitivity—what all Christian parents hope to instill in their children. And I felt blessed to be witnessing it in Christopher at such a young age. That day God spoke to me through my son and showed me not only what I needed to change but also a truth that warms any mother's heart: that my children really *are* hearing what I'm teaching.

Even though motherhood doesn't pay a salary, it pays in ways that far exceed a paycheck. Whenever my children learn something new—whether it's tying their shoes, sharing a toy without a fight, or growing in their love for Jesus each day—it's like a promotion for me.

As with any job, I have days I would love to sleep in or quit, but then my kids do or say the sweetest thing and my heart melts. I'm reinspired to get up and keep going. It's as if God, as my boss, gives me unexpected bonuses through the hugs and hearts of my children. He gave me this job; he knows I can handle it, and he sends encouragement when I need it most.

I'm learning that motherhood is about seeing crumbs on the floor and spots on the mirror . . . but leaving them while you play a game with your children or create a pint-sized masterpiece with colored paper, scissors, and glue. My house may not be perfectly kept. But I hope my children will remember that I made a haven of our home—and that I loved my job.

ROBIN TURNER

Words of Life

A glad heart makes a happy face; a broken heart crushes the spirit. *Proverbs 15:13* 🍂 Teach your children to choose the right path, and when they are older, they will remain upon it. *Proverbs 22:6* 🍂 Always be full of joy in the Lord. I say it again— rejoice! *Philippians 4:4*

LIVING IT OUT

If it sometimes seems you are getting nowhere with your child rearing, don't give up. Keep the faith, choose to maintain a positive attitude, and stay in the Word—it's our guide for every problem. Give your past failures to God. Keep your eyes focused on the future, and believe that God will bless your faithfulness as you train your children for his glory.

Drawing from the Well of Prayer

Dear God, please give me the grace and wisdom to train my children in such a way that their hearts will want to honor you. Help me to hold on to your Word as my guide in child rearing and in all of life. Thank you for being a loving, encouraging "Boss" to this sometimes weary but always grateful mother.

Carolyn Johnson

Carolyn is the wife of
Bishop Flynn Johnson,
the founder and senior elder of the
Atlanta Metropolitan Cathedral
in Atlanta, Georgia. An elder
herself, she is the founder
and president of the
Metropolitan Women's Summit.
Carolyn is also an accomplished
vocalist, lecturer, and teacher
on marriage and family
relationships.

Honesty—The Best Marriage Policy

As a pastor's wife in Atlanta's inner city, I've frequently had to assume the role of mentor and mama to the young women of the area. Since most of them don't have any role models for healthy relationships, they often ask me how I've been able to stay happily married for thirty years. Flynn and I have an excellent relationship. It's a gift from God, but we've also needed to work at it.

One of the things my husband and I agreed on a long time ago is that our relationship is only as strong as the things we are willing to talk about. We've found that if we work on and fight for our friendship and for a transparency between us, then the rest will come easier.

Over our years together, Flynn and I have discovered that the really daring call of the Spirit of God is for couples to talk about the things they've been afraid to talk about in the past. Why? Because the enemy is doing all he can at this hour to destroy marriages, and keeping things hidden from each other will only weaken the marriage. Instead, we need to find constructive ways to bring hard topics and feelings out in the open.

I remember one time, after twenty-three years of marriage, when I told my husband about a need that I had. "Flynn," I said, "I need a vacation."

"Great!" he said. "Where should we go?"

"No, you don't understand," I replied. And then, even though I wasn't sure what his reaction would be, I plunged ahead. "I need a vacation by myself, without you, the children, the responsibilities of home and church—everything." Flynn was startled at first, maybe even a bit hurt, but he came around quickly and decided to support me wholeheartedly in meeting that need.

Another step toward transparency is to be honest about how our monthly cycles affect us emotionally and physically. Many women have mood swings during these times, and those can adversely affect a marriage. I tell the men in our church, "Buy a calendar. It's one of the most powerful tools you can have." When a man knows where his wife is emotionally, it saves a lot of confusion and misunderstanding and helps him minister to her more effectively.

My husband often asks me a simple but powerful question, and it does wonders for our communication and connection: "What do you need me to do?" I love that. It frees me to ask him to do anything, from speaking the Word of God over me to giving me affection without any anticipation of a reward.

Finally, as you seek to develop an honest, loving relationship, remember to "fight fair" when resolving differences with your spouse. This means you need to be truthful about your thoughts and emotions. It means you attack the issue or the action, not the other person. And it means not going to bed angry. Be mindful that even if both of you are angry, your hearts want to reconnect. Take the initiative to reach out with honesty and humility. Your attitude will help defuse the situation and keep your union strong. As you work at keeping the lines of honest communication open, you'll strengthen your marriage and provide a defense against the enemy's destructive strategies.

WORDS OF LIFE

Who can find a virtuous and capable wife? She is worth more than precious rubies. Her husband can trust her, and she will greatly enrich his life. . . . Her children stand and bless her. Her husband praises her. *Proverbs 31:10-11, 28* 🐝 Any kingdom at war with itself is doomed. A city or home divided against itself is doomed. *Matthew 12:25* 🐝 Submit to one another out of reverence for Christ. *Ephesians 5:21*

Living It Out

Share the thoughts from this devotion with your husband. Talk about your desire to have a strong marriage that values honesty and "fighting fair." Ask him if he'd be willing to emphasize transparent communication and resolving differences in ways that would build up your marriage rather than tear it down. If you've withheld things from your husband that you now feel you should share with him, ask God for wisdom and sensitivity in doing so.

Drawing from the Well of Prayer

Father God, I'm thankful that you desire my marriage to be strong, honest, and loving. It's not always easy or comfortable to share my deepest thoughts and feelings with someone else—even with my husband. Please show me ways in which I can minister to him and do all that I can to make our home a safe haven for sharing our hearts with each other and working to create a strong relationship marked by honesty and humility.

CAROLYN JOHNSON

Cathy Lechner

Cathy speaks and ministers
internationally in addition
to serving alongside her
pastor-husband, Randi.
She is the author of numerous
books, including *I Hope God's
Promises Come to Pass before My
Body Parts Go South;
I'm Trying to Sit at His Feet,
but Who's Going to Cook Dinner?*
and *Couldn't We Just Kill 'Em
and Tell God They Died?*
Cathy and her husband are the
parents of seven children and
live in North Florida.

Humble Pie Isn't Too Bad—
It Tastes like Chicken

When I returned from my first missions trip, I got a firsthand look at how much religious pride was in me. On my first Sunday back home, I found myself being critical of the church. The people here had air-conditioning, but did they appreciate it? Oh no! Look at everyone glancing at their watches. The poor Filipinos didn't care how long you preached; they wanted all they could get of God and his Word. In fact, most of them didn't even own a watch. On and on I judged. From the padded pews to the short and tidy sermon, I judged.

But later that day the Holy Spirit checked my own attitude . . . and revealed my own pride. I couldn't help but wince. I'd been caught in the act. That's when I realized that pride isn't so much interested in getting things done for God as it is in letting others know what we did and how much we did. It's totally preoccupied with our image before others. In other words, we feel the need to let others know that God is using us just a little more than he's using someone else.

The greatest message on the spirit of pride that I've heard came from Pastor Jim Cymbala, of the Brooklyn Tabernacle in New York City. As he preached, he made an amazing statement: "Pride has the eternal hostility of God. God resists [pride] as a general in full battle array to bring you down." This was his interpretation of 1 Peter 5:5: "God sets himself against the proud, but he shows favor to the humble."

How true Pastor Cymbala's words are! When God looks down and sees pride, he smells the scent that ruined heaven, a scent very displeasing to him. And when I look at my own life, I can easily see the times when pride separated me from people I loved and ruined relationships that God had given to me. Perhaps if I'd just been willing to say "I'm sorry" or to try one more time to humble myself and change my opinions, I could have saved a friendship, avoided an argument, or resolved a difficult situation.

It's frightening when you look at Scripture and see the roll call of those who lost everything because of pride. Lucifer lost his exalted position in heaven; Nebuchadnezzar lost his kingdom; and Moses lost his chance to enter the Promised Land.

On the other hand, the Bible says clearly that God gives grace to the humble. We know that grace is the unmerited favor of God, but we need to see it as the gift we receive in exchange for giving up our pride. Everything we need for life is contained in God's grace. As we humble ourselves, we will receive the grace that contains power, love, wisdom, and God's leading.

Words of Life

Pride leads to disgrace, but with humility comes wisdom. *Proverbs 11:2*   Pride goes before destruction, and haughtiness before a fall. *Proverbs 16:18*   [The Holy Spirit] gives us more and more strength. . . . As the Scriptures say, "God sets himself against the proud, but he shows favor to the humble." *James 4:6*

Living It Out

Ask the Holy Spirit to reveal to you areas in which you have walked in pride, contention, and unforgiveness. He will show you! Be quick to repent and ask for the Lord's forgiveness and the forgiveness of others if he leads you to do so. Seek him earnestly in learning how to walk in humility and the fear of the Lord.

Drawing from the Well of Prayer

Dear God, please reveal any pride in me that hinders my relationships with other people and with you. Please replace my pride with a spirit of humility so I may readily rejoice in what others are doing for you instead of competing with them or judging them.

Cheryl K. Miller

Cheryl K. (Ewings) Miller,

a freelance writer,

lives on a lake in Georgia

with her youth-pastor

husband, Steve,

and a newly blended family

of seven sons.

When Depression Hits Home

Have you ever had one of those days when it takes tremendous effort just to drag your body out of bed? I had "one of those days" that lasted months before I determined something was drastically wrong with me.

At first I told myself I had good cause to be blue. When my marriage of eighteen years dissolved in a painful battle, I felt emotionally drained. The disruption in our home caused my children to react negatively both at home and at school. Then my job, usually an island of peace in a chaotic, roiling ocean, added stress because my workplace moved to a new location, adding an hour-long commute to my day. My life was a shambles!

I felt overcome by hopelessness and despair and often found myself wide awake at 3:00 A.M., worrying about my future. My eating habits changed drastically—I now had to force myself to eat. I made stupid mistakes and even bounced checks for the first time in my life. Nap time after work had become a critical part of my day, but I knew I was really in deep trouble when I needed to lie down between showering and getting dressed for work in the morning!

What's wrong with me? I repeatedly wondered. *Am I losing my mind?*

My sister helped me climb out of this muddle by mailing me a book titled *Happiness Is a Choice,* by Drs. Frank Minirth and Paul Meier and others. Because my sister had suffered a biologically based depression a few years earlier, she recognized the symptoms of my pain, doubt, and despair. After taking the book's quick depression inventory, I discovered a partial answer to my strange symptoms. I wasn't crazy—I was *depressed!* I needed to see a doctor.

One of the toughest calls I've ever made was to schedule an evaluation by a psychiatrist at a local Christian clinic. I remember my panic and breathlessness, and I had to force myself to keep the appointment. Although my life didn't change overnight, gradually I began to feel normal. While the stresses of being a single working mother were still there, I now felt more able to handle them without deadly despair.

Many things combined to help me out of that deep pit: a small dose of an antidepressant, counseling, and a steadfast faith in God's love. During that time I found a friend in the psalmist David, who pours out his despair to God with gut-wrenching honesty. His psalms were a reminder that even when God seems far away, I am never outside his loving care.

Since treatment, my life has taken on a new peacefulness. I've developed a newfound faith in God's goodness and grace, despite my circumstances. I've traveled a long way since the deep despair of the early months after my divorce, but I know my journey isn't yet over.

If you or someone you know is living in the pits, don't wait to seek treatment, even if you have to get someone to help you do so. And remember, even when you can't feel him, God is waiting to help you through your sorrow and pain. He did it for me—and he'll do it for you, too!

WORDS OF LIFE

Why am I discouraged? Why so sad? I will put my hope in God! I will praise him again—my Savior and my God! Now I am deeply discouraged, but I will remember your kindness. *Psalm 42:5-6* 🐟 Despite all these things, overwhelming victory is ours through Christ, who loved us. *Romans 8:37* 🐟 O Lord, you have examined my heart and know everything about me. You know when I sit down or stand up. You know my every thought when far away. . . . I can never escape from your spirit! I can never get away from your presence! If I go up to heaven, you are there; if I go down to the place of the dead, you are there. If I ride the wings of the morning, if I dwell by the farthest oceans, even there your hand will guide me, and your strength will support me. *Psalm 139:1-2, 7-10*

LIVING IT OUT

If you struggle with depression, you're not alone. One in four women will wrestle with the energy loss, poor concentration, altered appetite and sleep habits, hopelessness, anxiety, and sometimes even suicidal tendencies associated with this debilitating condition. Yet despite the widespread nature of depression, some still fear the stigma attached to those who suffer from it or choose to seek help. But don't suffer alone! Check out the symptoms of depression. Find a Christian psychiatrist who can help you evaluate your symptoms and decide what treatment is appropriate, whether it be medication, involvement in a support group, changes in nutrition and exercise, or other steps that God can use to begin to lift you out of the dark place in which you find yourself. Although it may feel as if God is not there, he hasn't forsaken you. Cry out to him. He understands what you are feeling, and he can help you find hope, healing, and the desire to begin to live passionately again.

Drawing from the Well of Prayer

Thank you, Lord, for never moving away from my side, even when I can't feel you there. Help me to determine the best way to climb out of the pit of depression and discouragement I'm in. Give me the courage to get the assistance I need, no matter what anyone else says. How glad I am that even when my world is shifting and clouds of despair obscure my sense of your presence, you are still there. Your love is constant and abiding.

Verla Gillmor

Verla Gillmor is a popular speaker, writer, and business consultant who lives in the Chicago area. She is the author of *Reality Check: A Survival Manual for Christians in the Workplace* and president of LifeChasers, Ltd. (www.lifechasers.org), an on-line resource for Christians in the workplace. Verla also spent fourteen years as an award-winning news anchor, reporter, and talk-show host for Chicago radio affiliates of NBC, CBS, RKO Radio, and Mutual Broadcasting. She continues to be a frequent contributor to both Christian and secular magazines.

Need a Confidence Boost?

When I asked a friend who was riding in my car, "What do you like about yourself?" we rode in silence for several minutes. Finally she turned to me and said, apologetically, "I can't think of anything."

I was stunned. My friend is intelligent, charming, and compassionate, yet she couldn't see any of that in herself. I know she's not alone. Despite God's assurance that he's absolutely crazy about us, most of us can't believe he means *us*.

I can relate. I was a reporter for twelve years, and one of the first things I learned about researching a story was "garbage in, garbage out." In other words, if your raw data is flawed, you'll end up with a faulty conclusion. The same is true about how we see ourselves. If we lack confidence, maybe we're working with flawed data.

The reality is, in hundreds of subtle ways our culture, our family, our friends—even our thought life—all conspire to undermine our confidence. We may have grown up in families where we received no affirmation, encouragement, or respect, the building blocks to self-confidence. Then we found ourselves smack-dab in the middle of a world that lionizes size-two Hollywood starlets and Barbie-doll figures. Our paychecks, titles, designer labels, and many other artificial yardsticks give us temporary entrée into the world of The Accepted. But in our hearts, we know it isn't real.

So how can we gain the confidence that God wants us to have?

Name the lies—and give them to God. Make a list of the falsehoods that others have said about you and what you've believed about yourself. Be specific. Then agree with God that that is not how he sees you. Focus your attention on God, who can change you from the inside out.

Grieve the loss of what you'll never have and never be. I once knew a woman who felt as if the world always let her down. Eventually, however, she confessed to God the truth—playing the victim was easier for her than dealing with her own emotional "junk." In my case, I had to grieve the loss of having only one child when I wanted a whole houseful.

Replace the lies with the truth. God's Word is full of information about your identity and your position as a believer in Jesus Christ. Let the wonder of God's perspective on you soak in. Did you know that you are

- fearfully and wonderfully made (Psalm 139:14)
- precious to God (Isaiah 43:4)
- cared about since your conception (Isaiah 46:3)
- God's child (John 1:12)
- Jesus' friend (John 15:15)
- chosen by Jesus (John 15:16)
- loved dearly by God (John 16:27)
- free from condemnation (Romans 8:1)
- a temple—a dwelling place—of God's Spirit (1 Corinthians 3:16)
- redeemed and forgiven of all your sins (Colossians 1:14)

When you realize fully what this means, you will know beyond a shadow of a doubt that you have incomparable value and that you are worth the sacrifice of what was most precious to God—his only Son. God may be the only Person you'll ever know who loves you unconditionally. But once this truth soaks in, God's opinion becomes the only one that matters.

WORDS OF LIFE

God created people in his own image; God patterned them after himself; male and female he created them. . . . Then God looked over all he had made, and he saw that it was excellent in every way. *Genesis 1:27, 31* Don't copy the behavior and customs of this world, but let God transform you into a new person by changing the way you think. Then you will know what God wants you to do, and you will know how good and pleasing and perfect his will really is. As God's messenger, I give each of you this warning: Be honest in your estimate of yourselves, measuring your value by how much faith God has given you. *Romans 12:2-3*

LIVING IT OUT

Are you sabotaging your own confidence? Ask yourself the following questions:

1. What judgments do I make about myself that are untrue? What is something wonderful about me that I have undervalued?
2. How do I typically respond when someone praises me? Is it hard for me to receive a compliment? If so, why?
3. Do I fail to stick up for myself when someone challenges what I know to be true?

If these questions reveal that you *are* sabotaging yourself, then reread the Scripture verses above to help you replace the lies with God's truth.

Drawing from the Well of Prayer

God, I know you made me—and you don't make junk. Help me to see the lies I have been believing for what they are—lies—and then get rid of them. I want to see myself the way you see me, as your precious child. Please begin the process of changing my mind and my heart so your opinion is the only one that truly matters to me.

Elizabeth Cody Newenhuyse

Elizabeth Cody Newenhuyse is
managing editor of *Moody* magazine,
the author of several books,
and a conference and retreat speaker.
She lives with her family
in the Chicago area.

Cultivating Contentment

There's a lot in my life I wish I could change. I'm not miserable—but I struggle with being satisfied.

One Scripture verse that makes me squirm is the apostle Paul's reminder to Timothy: "If we have enough food and clothing, let us be content" (1 Timothy 6:8). I have food, but too often it's macaroni and cheese. I have clothing, but looking through the L. L. Bean catalog brings out my most materialistic urges. I have furniture, but it resembles estate-sale treasures more than it does Crate and Barrel chic. Often I'd like more—and better. And that's just the beginning of my discontentment.

I've met other women who struggle with the same conflict. My neighbor Jackie, the mother of teens, tells me her level of contentment fluctuates all the time. "It depends on our finances, the state of the house, my husband's and kids' moods, and whether or not I have PMS," she says.

Discontent can take a variety of forms. One is Jackie's vague sense of disequilibrium—sometimes she likes her life, and sometimes she doesn't. Another form is a more profound restlessness, like that of a single-parent friend who'd love to pull up stakes and move to Florida after her youngest is through school. But a third, more destructive discontent is that "never enough" spiral many of us get caught in—always wanting a bigger house, more money, a more prestigious job.

The problem is, many of us define contentment as that ideal state of constant happiness where every problem is solved and every goal is met. But what happens when you achieve a goal? It's like yanking dandelions—you pull one, and another pops up in its place.

ELIZABETH CODY NEWENHUYSE

Ten years ago I had a certain sum in mind as my ideal annual income. I thought, *If only I could earn that, my financial woes would be over*. Well, guess what happened when I reached that magic number. It no longer seemed ideal, thanks to inflation. In fact, it seemed pitifully inadequate. What I had thought would give me contentment didn't satisfy me any longer.

We're fooling ourselves if we think we'll ever solve all our problems this side of eternity. New dreams will always replace the old. Ultimately there's no true contentment apart from knowing, loving, and desiring to follow Christ.

If we're honest, most of us can't say we're content in every situation, as the apostle Paul learned to be (Philippians 4:12-13). But it *is* a model to aspire to.

We may never achieve absolute contentment. But as we seek God's peace and ask his help in setting our minds on "things above"—no matter what the world may throw at us—we may be able to say, echoing the apostle Paul, "I *am learning* to be content in every circumstance." Such thoughts will help you get over "never enough" and be satisfied with "what is."

Come to think of it, that would make a great inscription for a plaque. I could hang it in my kitchen and meditate on it as I start boiling the macaroni for dinner.

Words of Life

Set your minds on things above, not on earthly things. *Colossians 3:2, NIV* I know how to live on almost nothing or with everything. I have learned the secret of living in every situation, whether it is with a full stomach or empty, with plenty or little. For I can do everything with the help of Christ who gives me the strength I need. *Philippians 4:12-13* Let the peace that comes from Christ rule in your hearts. For as members of one body you are all called to live in peace. And always be thankful. *Colossians 3:15*

LIVING IT OUT

How can you move closer to contentment in your life? Try these tips:

- Use a spiritual "measuring stick." If you feel uneasy about something, it may be a sign you're discontented with that situation.
- Give thanks. When you realize how much God has given you, you move closer to contentment. Look around you. What are you thankful for? The possibilities are endless. Each day, think of five new things to thank God for.
- Arm yourself against the seductions of the world. Reflect on the difference between "wants" and "needs." Don't get trapped by a desire to "have it all." Before you go shopping, pray for protection from the temptation to buy things you don't really need.
- Look beyond yourself. Don't limit your focus to your own needs and problems. Anything that stretches you, expands your world, or helps you share yourself with others will help to foster contentment.

Drawing from the Well of Prayer

Lord, the world is sometimes so much "with us." Help me to set my mind on "things above" rather than on "things below." Teach me to be content in every circumstance because I know all things in my life are governed by you. Amen.

Kathy Troccoli

Singer-songwriter Kathy Troccoli's
classic first album, *Stubborn Love*,
was completed four years after she
became a Christian. Kathy, who has
received two Dove Awards, has appeared
on *The Tonight Show* with Jay Leno,
Live with Regis and Kathie Lee, and
Entertainment Tonight. As a spokesperson
for Prison Fellowship, a Houston-based
AIDS organization called His Touch
Ministries, and Life Teen, a Christian
organization for youth, Kathy has
challenged people of all ages to a deeper
commitment to Christ. Her Baby's Prayer
Foundation raises financial support and
provides grants to life-affirming
organizations. She has appeared at
Women of Faith, Heritage Keepers, and
Time Out for Women Only conferences
and has written two books, *My Life Is in
Your Hands* and *Different Roads*.

When Everything Changes

I've always been sensitive to people who are hurting. Even as a child I was highly emotional and felt life deeply.

When I was sixteen, my dad died of colon cancer. And then, at a crucial time in my recording career, my mom was diagnosed with cancer. There were nights when I lay in bed and cried out to God, *Why did I lose one parent and now have to lose another?* Even as a grown woman I felt like an orphan.

Through the long months and years of reflecting on the pain, I knew I had to make a decision about my own response. If I chose bitterness, I'd miss the comfort God would send my way through myriad surprises. But if I chose to follow Jesus through the pain and believe his promises in the midst of it, I'd have hope, even if I didn't know what was ahead.

A comment from a close friend really helped: "Kathy, remember that your circumstances have absolutely nothing to do with God's ability to fulfill his Word. God is always sovereign, always in control . . . even when everything in life changes."

I chose to hold on to God's hope. But it didn't mean that the process of watching my mother die was easy. Far from it. I choked back tears as I sat beside her day after day in the hospital room, holding her hand and reading her the Psalms. And I was gratified to see her own relationship with Jesus growing closer, knowing that soon they would be walking hand in hand.

Then, just when my song "Everything Changes" became a top hit, everything in my life changed as well. My mother died, and I was left an orphan. Then death also struck others I loved. My grandmother died two months later and my grandfather four months after that.

The very underpinnings of who I was seemed to disappear, and my life became even more uncomfortably unpredictable.

In the darkness of that time, however, I discovered an awesome truth that now rings deeply and loudly in my soul: Life will always be unpredictable. You can count on that. But you needn't walk alone. God is the only source of true security. People and things won't remain, but God will. And because of that, now I continually examine myself to see where my sense of worth is coming from: my accomplishments, other people's opinions—or God.

Because of the losses in my life, my soul continues to cry out ultimate, burning questions about the things that will matter most in the long run: Am I loving well? Do I show genuine love and concern for others? Am I treating them as precious in my sight and in God's sight? Are the virtues of Jesus—his purity, humility, mercy, and kindness—such a part of my character that when people look in my eyes or hear my voice, they see or hear Jesus? Does the light in my soul point them toward God?

I continually pray that God will increase my hunger for godliness so that in some small way the people I meet will want to take a second look at Christianity—and the God who longs to interact intimately with our souls.

WORDS OF LIFE

The Lord is my rock, my fortress, and my savior; my God is my rock, in whom I find protection. *Psalm 18:2* [Jesus said,] "I am leaving you with a gift—peace of mind and heart. And the peace I give isn't like the peace the world gives. So don't be troubled or afraid." *John 14:27* Jesus Christ is the same yesterday, today, and forever. *Hebrews 13:8*

Living It Out

Do you feel like an orphan—emotionally, physically, or spiritually? Most of us do at some time in our lives. If this is such a time for you, go to God. Thank him first for the ways he has worked in your life, for the good things you have received. Then pour out your heart to him about how you are feeling. Are you struggling with singleness? the death of a loved one? an unbelieving spouse? illness? Whatever your situation, ask God to bring into your life people who will support you and give you comfort, wise advice, and most of all, listening ears.

Drawing from the Well of Prayer

Father, I know in my head that all things are sifted through your hands, but sometimes my heart has a hard time remembering. Thank you for your many blessings—and for those I sometimes forget to count. Help me in this time of darkness to keep my eyes focused on your light and your eternal love.

Beth Moore

Author and Bible teacher Beth
Moore's passion—and the mission
of Living Proof Ministries—
is to promote biblical literacy
and help people love God's Word.
She has an extensive speaking
schedule and is the author of
numerous books and Bible studies,
including *A Heart Like His*, *Breaking
Free*, and *Feathers from My Nest*.
Beth is a graduate of Southwest Texas
State University. She and her
husband, Keith, have two daughters
and live in Texas.

Bitter or Better?

On September 11, 2001, our world changed—externally and internally. For several centuries our nation has been like the people of Israel released from the bondage of Egypt. Like them, our forefathers crossed the sea to worship their God in liberty. For more than two hundred years we've celebrated our deliverance much like the children of Israel did.

Now we, like the children of Israel, stand at the bitter waters of Marah. Some of us stand on the shore and mourn for those who mourn. Others of us are waist-deep in the waters of personal tragedy and inexpressible loss: A mother who lost both husband and son. A husband who lost both wife and unborn child. A fiancée who waited for her groom to emerge from the ashes because their wedding date was a few short weeks away and she didn't want him to be late. We stand at the waters of Marah. The taste is bitter. And we are so tempted to drink.

No foe can defile you like bitterness. Its roots push their way through the most determined ground. So how can you defend yourself against it? Hebrews 12:15 says, "See to it that no one misses the grace of God and that no bitter root grows up to cause trouble and defile many" (NIV).

The grace of God doesn't come in prepackaged, one-size-fits-all containers. His grace is given according to our need. His mercies are new every morning. They belong to us by the Cross of Christ. Oh, that we would allow God to plunge the wood of the cross into our bitter waters so that one day—*one day*—the waters will be sweet. Oh, that our pools of tears would become springs of revival!

God made a profound promise to his children in Exodus 15:26: If they would just listen to him and do what was right, they would not take on the diseases of the Egyptians. Today our enemy isn't the Egyptians; our enemy is terror. And he is diseased with hatred, scorn, violence, and an insatiable thirst for blood. Oh, that we would not catch his diseases. The most profound threat is not that we might catch the diseases the terrorists flew over this country to bring us. The most profound threats are the insidious diseases sent to attack both heart and soul. *That* is what you must defend yourself against.

The grace not to become bitter—no matter what lies ahead—is yours if you want it. Crises invariably cause preoccupation. You cannot continue on with business as usual. You are changed. You must mourn. You must think. To be untouched right now could mean only that you are pitifully out of touch—with your own emotions, with your fellow creatures. Yes, these are days of preoccupation. As a nation, we cannot help it. But you can decide where to direct your own preoccupation. If you focus on your enemies, you will undoubtedly catch their diseases. But if you choose to fix your gaze on God, if you incline your ear to his voice and do what is right even when others do what is wrong, you will be healed. That is a promise. For he is the Lord who heals you . . . and he can heal a nation, too.

Words of Life

Get rid of all bitterness . . . as well as all types of malicious behavior. Instead, be kind to each other, tenderhearted, forgiving one another, just as God through Christ has forgiven you. *Ephesians 4:31-32*   The eyes of the Lord search the whole earth in order to strengthen those whose hearts are fully committed to him. *2 Chronicles 16:9*   You keep track of all my sorrows. You have collected all my tears in your bottle. You have recorded each one in your book.   Psalm 56:8

LIVING IT OUT

Each day you're faced with decisions—large and small—about whether to become bitter or better. Perhaps a husband or boyfriend has walked out of your life. Or you're struggling with the demands of a young child, a challenging job, or the constant heaviness of depression. Each time bitter thoughts begin to enter your thought life, pray immediately. Ask God to help you work *through* those situations, instead of asking him to always *remove* them. Then ask him to show you *his* will and *his* glory in the situation.

Drawing from the Well of Prayer

God our Healer, sometimes I am engulfed by the waters of Marah. They are bitter, and I find myself becoming bitter too. Help me consistently to make a choice, in times of evil, to fix my gaze on you, to listen to your voice instead of the bitter voices of those around me. Show me yourself, God. I ask for your healing.

BETH MOORE

Rhonda Redmon

Rhonda Redmon, the older
daughter of James and Betty
Robison, has traveled extensively
with her husband, Terry,
on LIFE's missions trips to war-
and disaster-ravaged parts of the
world. A busy mother, she
homeschools their four children.
Rhonda and her family live near
Fort Worth, Texas.

Living without the Answers

One day as I was disciplining my daughter, Laney, who was six years old at the time, I sent her to her room for a time-out. I told her I'd let her know when she could come out.

Laney looked at me and insisted, "Mommy, you need to tell me when I can come out because I know you're gonna forget I'm in here!"

"Laney, I promise I won't forget you!" I assured her. It was obvious she didn't like my answer. She began to throw a fit, crying simply because she wanted to know when she could come out instead of trusting that I'd let her know at the right time.

The minute Laney closed the door to her room, the Lord began to show me that this scenario with Laney was a picture of my own heart. Ever since I was a little girl, I've always been a question asker. I'm sure my parents grew weary of the hundreds of questions I could ask in a single day! And to this day, I still have so many questions that I ask the Lord, so many things I have yet to fully understand.

I am a diligent seeker for the truth. But while this is a great asset in my life, it can often bring me much pain. I may not throw a fit on the floor, but I can refuse to let my heart rest in the Lord and trust him when I don't get an immediate answer or gain complete understanding. Often if a question comes to mind and I don't immediately know the answer, in some ways I stop living. My joy begins to wane, and my mind becomes a circus of activity.

Yet Proverbs 3:5-6 says, "Trust in the Lord with all your heart and lean not on your own understanding; in all your ways acknowledge him, and he will make your paths straight" (NIV). To acknowledge him means to trust him, rest in him, even when you don't understand or when it causes you to be angry.

The truth is that we have a heavenly Father who loves us more than we could ever fathom. And he is more faithful to us as his children than we could ever dream of being to our own children. God has promised to show us everything we need to know, to mold us into his image, and cause the change in us. We must simply remain yielded to him and his purposes in our lives. Sometimes all we have to do is go to our rooms—get alone with God—and wait confidently for his answers. We can trust him; he'll *never* forget us.

Words of Life

Show me the path where I should walk, O Lord; point out the right road for me to follow. . . . Who are those who fear the Lord? He will show them the path they should choose. *Psalm 25:4,12*   Remember, the Lord is coming soon. Don't worry about anything; instead, pray about everything. Tell God what you need, and thank him for all he has done. If you do this, you will experience God's peace, which is far more wonderful than the human mind can understand. His peace will guard your hearts and minds as you live in Christ Jesus. *Philippians 4:5-7*

Living It Out

First, if you are a parent, ask God to teach you many wonderful things about your relation-ship with him through your children. Second, never allow unanswered questions to deter-mine your level of joy. Don't waste hours or days worrying about whether or not God is going to do his job! And last, if something needs to change in your life, trust God to show you—but don't stop living. God is faithful, and his love for you surpasses any love you have ever known.

RHONDA REDMON

Drawing from the Well of Prayer

Father, speak to me today. Help me walk in your peace. Please guide me and teach me all that your heart is longing for me to hear. Thank you for your ever-increasing faithfulness to me and to those I love. I trust you today, not just in times of rejoicing but also in times of discipline. You are a wonderful Father to me, and I'm forever grateful for your presence in my life.

Chonda Pierce

Chonda Pierce, a writer and national speaker, is known for her energetic, clean, humorous comedy routines, as well as her vocal talent. She has written several books, including *I Can See Myself in His Eyeballs*, *It's Always Darkest before the Fun Comes Up*, and *Second Row, Piano Side!* as well as audio products (*Chonda Pierce on the Soapbox* and *Having a Girls' Night Out*). Currently she's a main speaker at the Women of Faith conferences. She, her husband, David, and children, Chera Kay and Zachary, live in Tennessee.

Smiling through the Pain

People often think that a Christian home—especially one in which your father is a minister—should always be stable in times of adversity. But our family saw some very dark days, and although we are not of the world, we are still *in* the world, a place that can sometimes be very hard and unwelcoming.

I was a young teenager when my sister, who was twenty years old, was suddenly killed in a tragic car accident. When Charlotta died, a deep depression settled into my dad's spirit, and he began to sink into the gloom and despair of grief.

My parents' marriage began to waiver, and they eventually divorced. Then, about twenty months after we buried Charlotta, my little sister came home from high school with a sore throat. She was fifteen, beautiful, and a lot of fun. She was diagnosed with leukemia and died twenty-one days later.

My brother married and moved away shortly thereafter, so within less than a year and a half, my family of six dwindled to just Mother and me. We had to get out of the parsonage and out of the church that my dad had pastored because a new minister was coming to take his place. So, when I was eighteen, Mom and I moved to a one-bedroom apartment and started life all over again.

During this time, I often heard about "God's timing" and how "time" will take care of your hurts and pain. "In time, you will feel better about this," people would say to me. I always felt like saying, "Baloney!"

For me, time never did anything about the pain. I still hurt. The tears still came. And the grief I felt over the fact that my sisters would never know my children was all too real.

Eventually I learned that what you let happen in the aftermath of a dark time is what makes all the difference. You can sit and wallow in the bitterness of your hour, or you can get yourself up and take your pain to the foot of the Cross—and leave it there. I found that it's possible to let go of bitterness and grab hold of joy, and even laughter, in Christ. You can choose to let circumstances get the best of you, or you can say, "I'm going to be better for this," and move on.

I can't think of a better example of doing just that than my mother. While battling breast cancer, she began to have "no hair days" because of her chemotherapy. One day, with Mom wearing her new wig, she and I went to the cemetery to put flowers on the graves of family members. It was a very windy day. Now, nobody had told us about the tape that you can use to keep the "hair" on. So the wind blew her wig right off, and it rolled around wildly in the grass. I was trying to lighten the moment when I said, "Mother, you look like Yoda!"

Never having seen a movie in her entire life, she thought it was a compliment. As the hair tussled about like a tumbleweed, my poor mother yelled, "Are you going to help me catch this thing or not?" So we chased the wig, finally caught it, and shoved it back on her head. Covered with grass, it sat on top of Mom's head like a crooked mess. It looked terrible.

But Mom was laughing so hard that she had to sit down to catch her breath. When she had settled down, she said, "Well, as long as I can chase my hair, I guess I'm alive!"

I shook my head in disbelief and thought, *Man! This has got to be the power of Jesus. Who else could come into your life at the worst moment and give you such peace that you can laugh about something that would normally break your heart?*

CHONDA PIERCE

Words of Life

Give your burdens to the Lord, and he will take care of you. *Psalm 55:22* I will care for you. I will carry you along and save you. *Isaiah 46:4* Give all your worries and cares to God, for he cares about what happens to you. *1 Peter 5:7*

Living It Out

If you are walking through a dark period, remind yourself that it's important to allow yourself time to grieve and heal. Remember that you can choose to do things that will let you say, "I'm going to be better for having gone through this." Take your pain to Jesus, and ask him to redeem it. Ask him to send your heart on a healing journey that will result in replacing the pain with joy and even laughter. Seek wise counsel and the comfort of friends who love you.

Drawing from the Well of Prayer

Dear God, guide me with the light of your love and the warmth of your comfort as I walk through this dark passage. Help me remember that you care about what I'm going through, and give me an eternal perspective when the days seem long and gray. Restore to me the joy of your salvation.

Part Two

BODY

Betty Robison

Betty Robison cohosts the
LIFE TODAY television show
with her husband, James.
She is the mother of three children
and the grandmother of eleven.
She and James have been
married for forty years
and live in the
Dallas–Fort Worth area.

Threefold Fitness

I always keep a watchful eye on the trends of our society because I feel a responsibility to seek a higher authority on the opinions and messages the world's authorities are offering to us. I weigh their advice in light of the Word of God. One of my greatest concerns is the way the media has drawn our focus to an extreme and impassioned emphasis on the body. In fact, the role models of magazine ads and television programs have driven the average person to strive for an unrealistic image of thinness.

Not only have I seen what the world views as the perfect body, but my mirror has prompted me to measure myself by that standard on many occasions! However, God encourages me to step away from the world's measurement and use *his* measure and *his* image of the perfect body. He says I am "fearfully and wonderfully made" (Psalm 139:14, NIV) and I have been created in his image.

Since God refers to our bodies as temples of the Holy Spirit, I conclude that he considers the care of my body to be very important. So, after carefully considering what I've learned from fitness and nutrition experts, I developed a balanced maintenance plan for my body. I follow this plan in three areas of my life that I have found to be vitally linked together: emotional, spiritual, and physical.

Emotional. Did you know that proper care of your body can stimulate the other vital areas of your being? When I feel good physically, I become mentally and emotionally charged. If I don't take responsibility for my physical needs, I begin a downward mental and emotional spiral.

Spiritual. You may think you're just battling cravings and laziness, but you're really in a spiritual battle for the control of your body. It's a spiritual battle to overrule our wills and emotions when we crave foods that are bad for our bodies or ignore our body's need for exercise. No matter what our wills and emotions tell us, the truth is that too much of certain foods such as sugar, fat, and caffeine are harmful to our bodies, and our bodies need exercise in order to stay fit.

Physical. I love to go for long, brisk walks, and I target a goal of two or more miles, three to five days a week. I love to walk with a friend because it gives me great fellowship and encouragement on my journey to total fitness. If I'm walking alone, I converse with the Lord and listen as he tells me all the things "[I] need for living a godly life" (2 Peter 1:3).

Words of Life

You must worship no other gods, but only the Lord, for he is a God who is passionate about his relationship with you. *Exodus 34:14* 🌿 You may say, "I am allowed to do anything." But I reply, "Not everything is good for you." *1 Corinthians 6:12* 🌿 I am praying that all is well with you and that your body is as healthy as I know your soul is. *3 John 1:2* 🌿 *Additional Reading: 1 Corinthians 15:40-58*

Living It Out

There is a wealth of good information available to help you make good nutritional choices as well as proper exercise choices. Do some research, or see your doctor to make sure you have a good idea of how to eat and exercise properly for your age and weight. Establish personal goals in the areas of physical, emotional, and spiritual health. Find a "threefold fitness" partner who will encourage you on the road to reaching your goals.

Drawing from the Well of Prayer

Father, I know you want me to honor you with my body. I want to be your temple of holiness—to exercise self-control so my body is strong and healthy. I want to walk in the energy and power of your Holy Spirit. Help me to take every thought captive to the obedience of Christ and make the best choices for my emotional, physical, and spiritual health.

❧ ❧ ❧

Lisa Bevere

Lisa Bevere, a popular speaker
and radio and television guest,
is also the author of best-
selling books, including
Out of Control and Loving It,
The True Measure of a Woman,
You Are Not What You Weigh,
and *Be Angry but Don't Blow It!*
She lives in Colorado with
her husband, John, also an
author of best-selling books,
and their four sons.

Freedom from "Self"

One day while I was in a tired, frazzled, quite unattractive state, I looked at myself in the mirror and seemed to hear the Lord tell me, "You are not who you see."

I argued, "I am *too* who I see!"

But I sensed him explaining, "It may be true that you feel tired, stressed, worn out, or fat, but that is not the truth about who you are. When you become empowered with the truth, then you can make decisions to leave the past behind and walk free from bondage to the image you have of yourself."

That day the Lord began to show me that the image I had of myself was who I became—not outwardly but inwardly. My desire to conform to the world's image of "the perfect woman," my longing for the approval of our culture, and my tendency to gauge my success or failure by the messages I received from the world's idols led only to inward bondage.

It's so easy to exchange God's view of "the perfect woman" for the world's view. Almost without exception the covers of secular women's magazines boast young, seductive women and promise to reveal the secrets to great sex, ageless beauty, and thinner thighs. The ultimate goal is self-gratification.

But God wants us to strip away the veil of self-worship. You may argue, "How could I worship myself? I have a bad self-image!"

I would answer, "Whenever you are focused primarily on your self-image and are limited by it, the image of self becomes your master."

God doesn't want us fulfilled through self; he wants us fulfilled through him. The Word of God is set up to reveal to us a good God. To feel good about ourselves, we have to be good.

Self-image is the defense mechanism we project while trying to protect who we really are. It's the projected image versus the protected one. Self-image is the image left vulnerable when we lose the innocence of self-unawareness.

Most of us lose the unconscious sense of our physical bodies and instead become tethered to a consciousness of our bodies that makes us feel uncomfortable. We lose consciousness of ourselves when we become more aware of God and his will than we are of ourselves and our wills. This is a work of the Spirit, accomplished as we begin to renounce our natural limitations and abandon ourselves to him.

God doesn't want us to seek fulfillment through the avenue of self—that's futile and destructive. He wants us to seek fulfillment in him by seeking and serving him and others. When we shift our focus from self to Savior, we will experience an ongoing heart-level transformation into his image.

Most Christian women want to be like the world but not part of it. God said through the prophet Ezekiel that he was grieved by Israel's "unfaithful hearts and lustful eyes that long for other gods" (Ezekiel 6:9). God wants to set us free from coveting what the world dictates as ideal. And that begins with an inward transformation that leads to freedom from the tyranny of self.

Words of Life

You made all the delicate, inner parts of my body and knit me together in my mother's womb. Thank you for making me so wonderfully complex! Your workmanship is marvelous—and how well I know it. *Psalm 139:13-14* All of us have had that veil removed so that we can be mirrors that brightly reflect the glory of the Lord. And as the Spirit of the Lord works within us, we become more and more like him and reflect his glory even more. *2 Corinthians 3:18*   Christ has really set us free. Now make sure that you stay free, and don't get tied up again in slavery to the law. *Galatians 5:1*

Living It Out

Guard yourself against allowing the images from magazines, billboards, and television to make you self-focused. Choose to believe God's truth about you. Look deeply into the loving eyes of the Lord, and let him transform your mind and heart into his image. Don't let a bad self-image keep you from fulfilling your goals and God-given destiny.

Drawing from the Well of Prayer

Dear Father, I want to be free and have the "unawareness" of a child again. Turn my focus away from me and toward you. Draw me close so I may see your face and feel your loving arms. Help me to tear down the idol of self and in its place build an altar to you.

Debbie Robison

Debbie, the daughter-in-law
of James and Betty Robison,
is married to Randy Robison.
Debbie earned her degree
in elementary education from
Oral Roberts University.
She and Randy have four
children and live in
Keller, Texas.

Faithful... or Fatigued?

Scripture tells us that we are to be faithful in the "little things." In my case, these "little things" are primarily "little ones." As a mother of four children, I find that my days consist mainly of "little things" like washing faces, folding clothes, and feeding mouths. Though it can be tedious, seemingly unrewarding work (kids are just as apt to complain about dinner as they are to show gratitude for it), the Lord tells us that these are the things upon which successful lives are built.

History, too, affirms the role of day-to-day motherhood. George Washington, Andrew Jackson, and Abraham Lincoln all attributed their success in life to their mothers' influence. It's hard to imagine that these mothers raised their sons knowing that they would be presidents, but that's just the kind of attitude mothers should have. They should want to do all they can to help their children succeed and be all that they can be. This requires ongoing commitment to daily tasks and attention to the details, or the "little things."

And this is true regardless of the roles in which we find ourselves. Whether we spend our days at home, in an office, on the mission field, or anywhere else the Lord may lead us, we must identify the "little things" and then work to apply ourselves diligently to them. But that diligent attention to the ongoing day-to-day details can lead to weariness, even when we know we are doing exactly what God wants us to do.

When our first child was born, Randy and I decided that I would stay at home to raise our family. Four children later, the job is certainly full-time, but it is my calling, and I find it fulfilling. My oldest daughter, Abbie, tends to do her homework on time. She has a natural interest in reading, writing, and learning, and I try to inspire her with creative ideas that will challenge and stimulate her.

My oldest son, Alek, on the other hand, doesn't have the same built-in drive to learn and study, so I am always looking for new ways to encourage, motivate, and praise him. I know that by paying attention to the "little things" in both of their lives, they will excel in their learning, and in the end, their success will be my reward.

At the same time, the "little things" that require my daily devotion are repetitive "little chores"—washing clothes, making beds, picking up toys, or any of the other endless tasks that all mothers face. Perhaps your tedious tasks consist of filing the same reports every week, attending the same meetings, or dealing with a difficult coworker or an irritable family member on a regular basis. Do we become weary of those "little things"? Of course! That's why we need to keep our eyes on our long-term goals. A mother's goals may be to see her children grow to mature and responsible adults who love God. For someone on the mission field, it may be the establishment of a vital body of new believers. As Christians, our ultimate goal is to please God. Keeping our eyes on that goal will help us to remain faithful in those ongoing "little things" when our bodies are weary and we are tempted to give in to fatigue. It has been said that "the devil is in the details," but the truth is that in faithfulness to the "little things," we are able to please God.

Words of Life

Commit yourselves wholeheartedly to these commands I am giving you today. Repeat them again and again to your children. Talk about them when you are at home and when you are away on a journey, when you are lying down and when you are getting up again. *Deuteronomy 6:6-7* The master was full of praise. "Well done, my good and faithful servant. You have been faithful in handling this small amount, so now I will give you many more responsibilities. Let's celebrate together!" *Matthew 25:21* God has given gifts to each of you from his great variety of spiritual gifts. Manage them well so that God's generosity can flow through you. *1 Peter 4:10*

LIVING IT OUT

You are a piece of art that God is designing and sculpting daily. He patiently and tediously gives his attention to chipping off your rough edges, keeping you on the proper path, and making you into what he wants you to be—an image of his Son. He pays attention to the smallest details, the "little things" in your life. As you follow his example, you too will find strength to continue to be faithful in the little things that fill your days.

Drawing from the Well

Father, you know so well what fills my days. You have given me special abilities to [fill in your roles], as well as share the gospel with those who have not heard it, and do whatever you have called me to do. Help me not to grow weary in accomplishing the little things that work together to fulfill your purposes for my life.

Lynn Vanderzalm

Lynn Vanderzalm, author
of *Finding Strength in Weakness:
Hope and Help for Families Battling
Chronic Fatigue Syndrome* and
*Spiritual Sunlight for the Weary:
Meditations for the Chronically
Fatigued*, has nearly recovered
from CFIDS and is able once
again to join her husband,
Bas, in serving the poor around
the world. Currently she is a
senior editor with Tyndale House
Publishers. Lynn and Bas have
two grown children and live
in Oregon.

Finding Strength in Weakness

Fourteen years ago, without warning, my immune system was hijacked by an illness that stripped me of 80 percent of my ability to function. Triggered by viral agents, chronic fatigue and immune dysfunction syndrome (CFIDS) left me battling pain, daily fevers, a crippling sleep disturbance, neurological dysfunction, and a fatigue so deep it was hard to walk from room to room. My situation was complicated by the fact that our daughter, nine years old at the time, became debilitated with the same illness, leaving her unable to attend school more than a few hours a week.

Life as I had known it came to a grinding halt. My type A personality was forced to become a type C: couchbound. That was hard for me. For most of my adult life I had been involved in "helping" ministries: teaching inner-city teenagers, working with homeless alcoholic men and women, teaching Bible studies, acting as an advocate for the needs of the poor. I gained satisfaction from what I did. But CFIDS changed that. Now I spent most of my days on a couch. Of what value was that?

I struggled with questions: Was I now an invalid, a "not valid" person? Had I lost my value to God and others?

Through my battle with this illness, I had to confront a false illusion head-on: that I could be useful to God only when I was in top shape, when I was whole. Once this illusion was stripped away, I began to realize that God can use broken, weak bodies as effectively as he can use healthy ones. What a revelation!

And God *did* use me—even in my physically broken state. Several women regularly came to sit at the end of my couch, where I was free to listen to their struggles and pray with them through difficult circumstances: a canceled wedding, painful infertility, shattered dreams, life with an alcoholic husband.

My life on a couch was valuable to these women because I had time for them, time undisturbed by busy schedules and activities. But more than that, my *illness* was valuable to them because they knew I understood pain, suffering, uncertainty, waiting, and unanswered questions. Together we experienced life without our normal props. Together we learned what it meant to cling to God alone. Together we prayed and waited.

Over time I came to believe that my value as a person lies not in what I do but in *who I am*. I'm just as valuable to God when I'm on a couch as when I'm behind a podium. What counts is not my accomplishments but my faithfulness to God's purposes in my life.

Through my illness, I've learned to trust that God can use suffering for his good purposes in my life and in the lives of others. I've learned to trust that his gifts to me are good, even if they do not come in packages that I recognize as gifts.

Words of Life

My grace is sufficient for you, for My strength is made perfect in weakness. *2 Corinthians 12:9, NKJV* You, Lord, are all I have, and you give me all I need; my future is in your hands. How wonderful are your gifts to me; how good they are! *Psalm 16:5-6, GNT* I have cheerfully made up my mind to be proud of my weaknesses, because they mean a deeper experience of the power of Christ. I can even enjoy weaknesses, sufferings . . . and difficulties for Christ's sake. For my very weakness makes me strong in him. *2 Corinthians 12:9-10, Phillips*

Living It Out

If you have been sidelined by difficult circumstances, make life-giving choices:

1. Choose to believe that God is good, even when your situation seems bad.

2. Choose to believe that God is in control, even when your life seems out of control.

3. Choose to see your weakness as a gift from God.

4. Read biographies of people who have survived life-threatening events. Learn from their courage, endurance, and faith.

5. Allow God to use your suffering, pain, and questions for his good purposes— to strengthen you and others.

6. Find other people who are walking a similar journey, and encourage each other along the way.

7. Do all you can to stay emotionally and spiritually strong: pray, study the Bible, share your struggles with mature Christian friends, and share your victories with other people who are weak.

Drawing from the Well of Prayer

Lord, you are good, and you are in control. You are my strength and my song. You are all I need. I thank you for your good gifts, even those that involve pain, suffering, and uncertainty. I thank you that in your grace you take the crumbs of my disappointments and transform them into bread that feeds and nourishes others. In the name of Jesus, the Suffering Servant, amen.

Kathryn S. Olson

Kathryn Olson, a senior editor of
women's fiction, has a bachelor's
degree in philosophy from
Northwestern University and
worked in Human Resources for
several years before finding her true
calling in the editorial field.
Baking, listening to classical music,
and watching football games are
pastimes she shares with her
husband, Timothy, who is a
professional violinist and avid
Minnesota Vikings fan.
The Olsons make their home
in Wheaton, Illinois.

The Empty Crib

It happened in the cereal aisle of my local supermarket. I ran into my third mother-and-baby pair of the morning, and grief blindsided me. Feeling as if I'd been punched in the gut, I dissolved into tears, hoping no one would notice.

I'd lost my only child to miscarriage more than a year and a half before. Although time and God's grace had gone a long way toward healing my heart, that morning reminded me that a mom never really gets over the loss of a child, even a preborn child. But there are ways to cope—and even to accept this difficult path God has set before me. If you or someone you care about is facing infertility, perhaps these suggestions will help.

1. *Be gentle with yourself.* Taking care of yourself may feel selfish, but sometimes we need a break from people and situations that hurt. I'm not suggesting you withdraw from life, but do cut yourself some slack. Whether the cause of renewed pain is a Mother's Day celebration, baby shower, or the passing of another monthly cycle without fulfilling your dream of motherhood, when you're feeling especially low, do something just for you. One of my favorite escapes is snuggling on the couch with an afghan, a bowl of popcorn, and a favorite book.

2. *Allow yourself to grieve.* Since the loss of my baby, funerals are especially stark reminders that God sometimes asks us to entrust our loved ones back into his arms. I even grieve that I was denied this comforting ritual of death—and celebration of a life—for my child.

But I draw great comfort from the simple power of John 11:35: "Jesus wept." I'm comforted to know that when my loss—or that of others—leads me to tears, I'm being Christlike. It's okay to grieve.

3. *Expect emotional ups and downs.* Grief comes in cycles. When the magnitude of my loss sank in—two months after my miscarriage—everyone else had already moved on with their

lives, and I felt funny talking about it. I've never been much of a crier, but since my miscarriage, grief blindsides me in unexpected places. I've learned that's normal, and I need to accept it.

4. *Embrace the life God has for you.* I still hope God will bring children into my husband's and my life someday—either through natural birth, adoption, or a combination of the two. But I choose not to focus on having a baby. I'm learning that true joy is found in submitting myself to God's plans for me . . . even when it hurts. I have to make a conscious effort—especially on my "weepy" days—to affirm my trust in a God who loves me and wants the best for me. C. S. Lewis expresses it well: "We are not necessarily doubting that God will do the best for us; we are wondering how painful the best will turn out to be."

5. *Look for God's comfort.* Even in the midst of pain, I've seen evidence of God's loving care, especially through understanding friends.

One morning, after I had cried myself to sleep the night before, my friend Beth sent an e-mail: "I've been praying for you—God woke me around 4:00 this morning, in fact, with you and Timothy and babies on my mind! I felt led to pray for your faith to increase."

Wow. Tangible evidence that God had not forgotten me. Beth's prayer was right on target. I need more faith that God's way is truly best, even when it doesn't line up with my desires. As a character in one of my favorite books says, "I just want to look more like Jesus when I get to the other side of this thing." I hope it will be with a baby in tow. But if not, I know that God still really does desire the best for me.

Words of Life

You keep track of all my sorrows. You have collected all my tears in your bottle. You have recorded each one in your book. *Psalm 56:8* The Lord will work out his plans for my life—for your faithful love, O Lord, endures forever. *Psalm 138:8*

LIVING IT OUT

Do you know someone who is struggling with the pain of a miscarriage or infertility? Here are some tangible ways to show your love and support that will almost always be welcome:

1. Give lots of hugs. Almost always, a hug is better than words.
2. Write notes of encouragement. These can be read and reread when a friend is having an especially hard day.
3. Acknowledge the loss. To be safe, avoid platitudes or advice. Express your love with simple statements like "I'm so sorry" or "I'm praying for you."
4. Be sensitive to your friend's feelings if you become pregnant or adopt a child. Don't complain about morning sickness or diapers. No matter how annoying these things might be to you, your friend would love to be in your shoes.

Drawing from the Well of Prayer

Lord, everywhere I go I see pregnant women or children in strollers, and yet my arms are still empty. I need your peace, Lord. You have promised to bind up the brokenhearted. Give me increased faith to believe that your purpose for me is perfect, even though it's painful. And use what you are teaching me to encourage others. In the name of the Gentle Shepherd, amen.

Elizabeth Mittelstaedt

Elizabeth Mittelstaedt is the editor
of *Lydia*, the largest Christian magazine
in Europe, published in German,
Romanian, and Hungarian. She speaks
internationally at womens conferences
and in 2001 was named International
Woman of the Year by International
Biographical Centre of Cambridge,
England. She and her husband, Ditmar,
live near Frankfurt, Germany.

One Woman's Choice

The other day I chatted with a woman who tends to leave her feelings unspoken and finds it difficult to say, "I love you." As we talked, I remembered a story she told me years ago about a young pregnant woman during the final stages of World War II. At the time, diphtheria was rampant in battered Europe, and like many others, this woman had succumbed to the disease. There was no medicine available, and having this child could cost her her life.

Should I have an abortion? she asked herself repeatedly as she stared out the window of a streetcar and shivered in the crisp air that spoke of a harsh winter to come. Despite the fact that the doctor's suggestion to abort seemed the wisest course of action, a sense of foreboding gripped her heart. *Do not kill,* a voice seemed to say.

The young woman looked around quickly. *Where did that come from?* she wondered. *Was it God?* She dismissed the thought rapidly. *How could it be? I don't even know him,* she told herself and continued her internal argument. *What chance does this child have to survive anyway? Does anyone care about one more baby?*

But the warning not to kill echoed in her thoughts, and the young woman changed her mind and went home without having an abortion. I'm glad—because that woman was my mother, and I was that unborn child.

Many years later, after my mother had become a Christian and told me her story, she added: "Remember, God watched over you even before you were born. God really loves you."

I've stored those words in my heart. I *am* special. God did care for me. Yes, he knew me even before I was born, as Psalm 139:16 says.

The end of World War II, with the epidemic and so many other uncertainties, wasn't a good time to bring a child into the world. Yet many other mothers have faced similar difficult circumstances.

One of these was Moses' mother. Jochebed made the courageous decision to save the life of her son at a time when no Jewish baby boys were allowed to live. And then there was Mary, the mother of Jesus, our Savior. Did her pregnancy come at a convenient time? No, the times in which she lived were difficult. But it was God's time for Jesus—and many years earlier, Moses—to be born.

Were you born at a difficult time for *your* mother? Have you aborted a child in the past? given birth to your own child during a difficult time? Are you adopted and are not sure who your biological parents are or why they "gave you up"? You may never know the answers to why you've had to go through such times—at least not on this earth. But there is a clear truth we can all live by: Life isn't always convenient, but God is always in control.

I've seen this truth work clearly in my own life. During a recent conversation my normally unemotional mother made a surprising statement. "Now that I'm old, I look back and am so glad to have you. You've brought a lot of joy to my life!"

I knew she wanted to say, "I'm glad I didn't abort you." But she didn't need to explain herself. In my heart I knew she was glad about the decision she had made that day on the streetcar.

How thankful I am for the two simple sentences she spoke. They warm my heart every time I think of them. And they have further encouraged me to think about how I can show love to my mother. I could fill pages with pretty prose and explain how much I appreciate her, but I believe I can best express the deepest thoughts of my heart in one sentence: "Mother, thank you that I am alive."

Words of Life

You made all the delicate, inner parts of my body and knit me together in my mother's womb. Thank you for making me so wonderfully complex! Your workmanship is marvelous—and how well I know it. You watched me as I was being formed in utter seclusion, as I was woven together in the dark of the womb. You saw me before I was born. Every day of my life was recorded in your book. Every moment was laid out before a single day had passed. *Psalm 139:13-16* [God said to Jeremiah,] "I knew you before I formed you in your mother's womb. Before you were born I set you apart." *Jeremiah 1:5*

Living It Out

What situations in your life—past or present—have been "inconvenient"? How have you felt in the midst of them? Unloved? Unlovable? Angry? Accepting? Bitter? Take some time to write God a letter about the situation. Tell him how you feel about the situation and what you're learning (for good and bad). Then ask yourself, *If I were put in this same situation in the future, what would I do differently next time, now that I know what I know?*

Drawing from the Well of Prayer

Father God, I admit it. Sometimes life—my life—is hard, and I wish things were different. In such times, help me to remember that you have watched over me all the days of my life, even before I was born, and that you have a special plan in mind just for me. Help me to be thankful for the gift of my life, even when times are stressful.

Marcia Van't Land

Marcia Van't Land is the author
of numerous devotionals, articles,
and anecdotes and has led
workshops and adult
education classes.
She and her husband, Tom,
have pastored two churches,
worked in campus ministry,
and have provided a home base
for college students and other
assorted people, including their
own three children.

Enough Faith?

In early 1980 I was a healthy thirty-two-year-old wife and the mother of three preschool children, as well as an athlete, teacher, and coach. I prided myself on being trim and in shape.

Then I spent a week in the hospital during a severe case of the flu. Afterward I went on with my busy family life, and we made a cross-country move. I blamed my fatigue and back pain on the fact that I wasn't getting enough rest. Then my feet began to flop when I walked, and I became nervous about holding my baby for fear of dropping her. Finally I went to a neurologist, who immediately put me in the hospital. My bladder and bowels stopped working. Ten days later the neurologist told me I had a rare disease called porphyria. As a result, today I'm in a wheelchair and have been hospitalized more than forty times.

When my good health disappeared, I mourned the loss of my ability to walk, to control the movement of my hands and arms. For a while I kept a stiff upper lip. Then, several years into my illness, I finally realized I no longer had the energy to protect my family and friends from my disease. I stopped pretending and let them see my struggle. Some I never saw or heard from again.

Others made insensitive comments: "If you had more faith, you wouldn't need that wheelchair." Such statements hurt deeply because at times I couldn't help but wonder the same thing. I doubt that I can bear this disease nobly.

However, after all these years of chronic pain I've come to see that losses in life are inevitable—and we must cultivate understanding, compassion, and courage in the midst of them. I've learned that my questions, when asked rightly, are signs of a deepening faith—that God

MARCIA VAN'T LAND

will provide what we need to grow beyond our tragedies if we trust him. That's why I tell people, "I believe that if and when God wants to heal me, he will."

There aren't always personal reasons for every problem in life. Unless God reveals some specific wrongdoing or a wrong pattern of living that has affected our health, it's not our business to draw connections between our medical problems and our standing with God. Sometimes we suffer simply because we have frail, human bodies.

Does that mean we shouldn't have faith and that we shouldn't believe in miracles? Of course not! God is capable of performing a miracle at any time or place. He has the power to accomplish his purposes over a period of time—or instantaneously. We don't know what God has in mind for us.

But I must trust that the condition I find my body in is one God can use. My faith reminds me that whatever situations I face, God will never forsake me and will give his comfort to me. I have a deeper relationship with God now than I did when I was healthy. I must rely on God completely, and when I do, he accomplishes his purposes beautifully in my life.

WORDS OF LIFE

When you go through deep waters and great trouble, I will be with you. When you go through rivers of difficulty, you will not drown! *Isaiah 43:2* If you are walking in darkness, without a ray of light, trust in the Lord and rely on your God. *Isaiah 50:10* Come to me, all of you who are weary and carry heavy burdens, and I will give you rest. *Matthew 11:28*

LIVING IT OUT

Grief is a process. And there are times when you *will* feel as if you've lost everything and everyone. You may wonder how you can go on. In such times, the following steps may help:

1. Recognize your need for help. Talk to a valued friend, gather a support group who understands your situation, seek outside and professional help.

2. Talk to God (even if all you can do is say, "Help me, God!").

3. Evaluate your physical condition. Make an appointment with a doctor if necessary.

4. Give yourself the positive boost of a new activity or hobby.

5. Get as much physical exercise as possible.

6. Don't get trapped by indecision. Make decisions and don't look back.

7. Take charge of your future. Set short- and long-range goals.

8. Reach out to others.

9. Let yourself cry.

10. Increase your laughter quotient. Try not to take yourself too seriously!

Drawing from the Well of Prayer

Dear God, thank you for walking alongside me in my suffering. Your Son wept at the death of Lazarus. He was kind to those who were grieving and didn't tell them to "snap out of it!" You see the whole picture of life, of which I am only a small part. How grateful I am that you are the King of the universe, the all-knowing Sovereign, the Almighty, and that you love me infinitely and know me intimately. In my own suffering, help me to remember that Jesus suffered too. And give me the courage to live out this verse every day: "Be strong and take courage, all you who put your hope in the Lord" (Psalm 31:24). Amen.

Joy Michaels

In order to protect her family relationships, Joy Michaels has written under a pseudonym. However, we applaud her for coming forward with this very difficult devotion. Statistics show that one out of five girls is sexually abused before she reaches adulthood (usually by a close relative). That number is likely to increase as long as society tolerates pornography—the impetus for sexual molestation, rape, and other crimes. Our prayer is that Christians will oppose pornography at every level— on the Internet, on television and movie screens, in bookstores, and in their homes.

Overcoming a Painful Past

It was a sunny afternoon, and my parents were at a church function when my thirteen-year-old brother called me into his bedroom and showed me some pornographic pictures. My eyes grew wide as he turned the pages. "You want to try it, just for fun?" he asked as he stuffed the magazine under his mattress.

I followed innocently as he led me to a twin bed stored in the basement and then fondled me. I was only seven.

For the next few years my brother periodically compelled me to meet him in his bedroom or in the basement. Confused and ashamed, I couldn't bear to tell anyone—especially my Christian parents. They trusted him implicitly, letting him baby-sit my four-year-old sister and me. My brother swore me to secrecy, and I felt the heavy burden of that secret.

None of my girlfriends at school knew much about sex, so I played dumb and put pressure on myself to appear normal. But at night I often cried and prayed that Jesus would let me die in my sleep so I could be with him in heaven.

When I turned eleven, my independent nature kicked in. Although I'd always felt ashamed about what was going on between my brother and me, I finally realized something was seriously wrong with his behavior. In a moment of courage one evening I turned down his advances. He stopped pursuing me for sexual stimulation, but I later learned that he went after my precious younger sister.

In high school and college I masked my fear and insecurity by getting high grades. Although I'd always wanted to remain a virgin until marriage, I wondered whether I still qualified. So when a college boyfriend pressured me into sex, I felt too defenseless to say no.

After graduation I drifted from my Christian upbringing, moved out of state, and continued to date guys who weren't good for me. I kept my secret well into my twenties, when I flew home to spend a weekend at my sister's house. While chatting, we revealed some of our painful childhood secrets, wondering with some self-pity and anger whether our relationship woes were somehow tied to our loss of innocence in childhood. Naively we encouraged each other to forgive, forget, and get on with life. I tried, but I didn't get very far.

I'd grown up hearing the gospel but had never considered a relationship with Christ. I soon surrendered my life to him and began to pray that God would restore my innocence and heal me from the abuse of my childhood. I craved justice and confronted my brother, but he denied his behavior. I told my dad, too, but he was too shocked to respond.

Eventually I saw a Christian counselor who tenderly prayed with me and through the Bible showed me that my view of God was incomplete. Yes, God was almighty and powerful, but he seemed unfamiliar and distant to me, not the heavenly Father who cared deeply for me. Over time my viewpoint began to change, and I began to deal with forgiveness toward my brother and my father. I began to accept that my family members might never respond the way I'd like, but God understands and has adopted me into his family (see Romans 8:15-18).

As I've grown in my faith, my desire to be vindicated has gradually disappeared, and my relationship with my parents has greatly improved. Despite the far-reaching ravages of pornography and sexual abuse, I no longer blame my brother for the botched-up decisions I made in adulthood. Instead, I pray that he will one day experience the forgiveness and grace I've experienced.

Through the Bible I've learned that I don't need to dredge up the sexual abuse from my past or hold a lifelong grudge against the one who stole my innocence. I don't even need to claim victim status. Why? Because I now understand that the same God who knit me together in my mother's womb allowed his innocent Son to suffer and be crucified—for my sins! Jesus has borne my griefs and carried my sorrows. Through his power, I can leave my past behind and focus on my Savior's love.

WORDS OF LIFE

The Lord is my light and my salvation—so why should I be afraid? *Psalm 27:1* 🐦 The Lord is close to the brokenhearted; he rescues those who are crushed in spirit. *Psalm 34:18* 🐦 I am focusing all my energies on this one thing: Forgetting the past and looking forward to what lies ahead, I strain to reach the end of the race and receive the prize for which God, through Christ Jesus, is calling us up to heaven. *Philippians 3:13-14*

LIVING IT OUT

Forgiveness is not a one-time event; it's a cycle. When memories of past abuses come to mind, turn these images over to God. Ask him to help you forgive that person—again. And then pray for the courage to move ahead with your life, acknowledging the realities of your past but resolving to make proactive, rather than reactive, decisions for your future.

Drawing from the Well of Prayer

God, sometimes I feel so worthless, ugly, and unclean because of the abuse in my past. I wonder whether anyone will ever truly love me. Remind me at such times that you are the unchanging One, that you know everything about me intimately and still love me. Help me to move ahead with purpose and joy.

Linda Mintle, Ph. D.

Linda Mintle is a psychotherapist who
writes for *Charisma, Spirit-Led Woman,*
and *Ministries Today* magazines.
She is the author of a number of books,
including *Getting Unstuck,* a book
dealing with women's issues, and has
also cohosted *The 700 Club.*

Trapped by Food

Weight matters to women. No matter how emotionally healthy you think you are, you may still obsess a little about your weight. Do you get a little depressed when you try on bathing suits in the spring? Have you ever lied about your weight on your driver's license? Are you dieting because of an upcoming wedding, class reunion, or other special event?

What about those yearly physicals when the nurse weighs us? We make sure to take off our shoes (that's another two pounds), our watch (it must be worth a few ounces), our earrings (a few more ounces), and our jacket (easily a pound). Stripped to the lowest common denominator—a flimsy, lightweight dress over underwear—we pray the scale will be kind.

Whom can we thank for our corporate neurosis? Lots of people, actually: our culture, our race and ethnicity, our socioeconomic status, ourselves, our families, and our biology. All of these factors influence our weight. The reality is that most of us don't look like the models in the *Sports Illustrated* swimsuit edition, and we probably never will. For all the money spent on weight loss, our society still has epidemic rates of obesity. Why in a society so health-and-fitness conscious are we still fat?

Part of the reason is that we eat tons of processed food, much of it high in fat and loaded with empty calories. We exercise little and spend much of our leisure time in front of screens—movies, TVs, and computers.

Some women see food as a friend and use it to fill emotional voids, calm anxiety, cover anger, protect themselves from sexual issues, and much more. Binge and compulsive eaters have often faced numerous losses in their lives (divorce, neglect, abuse, alcoholic parents, rejection, and loneliness), and they use food to soothe and protect themselves from pain.

Some women equate food with love. If you experience a lack of love, you can fill yourself with food. Food fills the empty places. But food obsessions also keep us stuck. Instead of dealing with life's losses and emptiness directly, we distract ourselves with food.

What's the answer? It's simple, but incredibly hard to do: learn to eat sensibly, begin to exercise, and stop using food as your emotional nurturer. Nourish yourself spiritually so that food holds less power over your life. Keep in mind that you don't need to be a slave to food. After all, God's love produces self-control. When we love God, we want to please him—in all areas of our lives. Bringing ourselves into obedience to his will for our lives also means disciplining ourselves. This may mean changing our behavior and addressing areas we've previously denied or numbed with food. To deal with these areas, you may need a therapist's help. If so, don't hesitate to get the help you need—no matter what others say.

Above all, as you work on all of the issues associated with your overeating, don't neglect filling yourself up with God's Word. Reading—and soaking in—God's love for you is the secret ingredient to any struggle with self-control, including overeating!

WORDS OF LIFE

Those who become Christians become new persons. They are not the same anymore, for the old life is gone. A new life has begun! *2 Corinthians 5:17* When the Holy Spirit controls our lives, he will produce this kind of fruit in us: love, joy, peace, patience, kindness, goodness, faithfulness, gentleness, and self-control. Here there is no conflict with the law. *Galatians 5:22-23* Humble yourselves before God. Resist the Devil, and he will flee from you. *James 4:7*

LIVING IT OUT

Ask God to show you how you are using food. Confide in a friend or a counselor, and brainstorm ways in which you can meet those needs without using food. Buy a cookbook of healthful recipes, and educate yourself about how to eat sensibly. Determine to exercise at least thirty minutes, three days a week. Even taking a brisk walk will boost energy, relieve stress, and lift your mood.

Drawing from the Well of Prayer

Dear God, I want to please you, and I want to stop being distracted by my weight and overeating. Please help me to hide your Word in my heart so that I make healthier choices for my body and my spirit. I'm thankful I don't have to be a slave to food. Please give me the perseverance to make whatever changes are necessary for me to gain freedom from food issues.

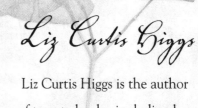

Liz Curtis Higgs

Liz Curtis Higgs is the author
of twenty books, including her
best-seller *Bad Girls of the Bible*,
five children's books, three novels
for women, and *Rise and Shine*.
Liz is also a columnist for
Today's Christian Woman magazine.
Since 1986 she has presented
more than fifteen hundred programs
in all fifty states and six foreign
countries, encouraging women and
helping them to grow in joy and
grace. Liz and her family live in
Louisville, Kentucky.

True Beauty

I had just stepped off the stage in Colorado Springs after experiencing a true "Rocky Mountain high" with a whole roomful of wonderful women. As I wove through the crowd, an enthusiastic attendee with a big grin stopped me.

"Liz," she began, clasping my hand in hers, "when I saw you walk out on the platform, I said to my friend, 'Hey, there's hope for us all!'"

I laughed out loud, realizing she meant no offense and also knowing how very right she was. If you've met me or seen my photo, you'd probably agree that in no way would I ever fit the standard description of a "platform personality." I'm not the right size, the right shape, or the right age for stardom. I'm not highly degreed (my bachelor of arts in English was earned after eighteen years and three colleges), and my favorite credentials are M.O.M.

So you see, the woman in Colorado Springs was correct: There *is* hope for us all. If Liz—with an overly abundant body, chemically dependent hair, and noncelebrity status—can muster enough confidence to speak for the Lord, then rest assured God can use you right now, "as is," if you'll just let him.

Some people call it "self-confidence," but I know better. At this point in my journey of faith, I've discovered that real confidence and beauty come from the Lord.

When we're looking at our own reflections in the mirror, we ask ourselves questions: "Do I look okay?" "Any problems that need fixing?" "Am I measuring up to expectations others have?" "Am I beautiful—even in a small way?"

But there's a problem with mirrors and with people: both can reflect a distorted picture of who we really are. Such images can be hurtful, unflattering, untrue, and just plain discouraging. That's why the best place to turn for an accurate picture of ourselves is the mirror of Scripture. That is the only way we can truly be beautified inside and out.

I know this beautifying process is legitimate because I've seen it happen again and again. When women come to know the Lord in a real and personal way, their frown lines begin to soften. A sparkle appears in their eyes, and a radiance falls over their countenance.

When you allow the Lord to fill your heart with his boundless love, it shows on the outside. This beauty has nothing to do with cosmetics or plastic surgery. On the contrary, it's an inside job: a heart full of love produces a face full of joy.

When I stepped into a church for the first time as an adult, I was amazed to see pew after pew of attractive women. *Is this a requirement of membership?* I wondered. *Maybe they're all Mary Kay consultants. . . .*

Soon I learned the happy truth: Such beauty and confidence are gifts from God. Unlike lipstick and blush, which seldom last longer than a few hours, spiritual beauty is timeless. It literally pours out of your pores and alters your appearance in a most pleasing way. People will think you've had a face-lift, when in fact you've had a *faith*-lift!

WORDS OF LIFE

All of us have had that veil removed so that we can be mirrors that brightly reflect the glory of the Lord. And as the Spirit of the Lord works within us, we become more and more like him and reflect his glory even more. *2 Corinthians 3:18* 🐦 Don't be concerned about the outward beauty that depends on fancy hairstyles, expensive jewelry, or beautiful clothes. You should be known for the beauty that comes from within, the unfading beauty of a gentle and quiet spirit, which is so precious to God. *1 Peter 3:3-4*

LIVING IT OUT

When you're lacking confidence for life's tasks, do a Scripture search of the names for God. You'll find that many of the names for people in Scripture are actually a reflection of the names of God: He is the shepherd; you are his sheep. He is the teacher; you are his disciple. He is the vine; you are the branches. As you look into the mirror of God's Word, you'll better understand your connection to Christ and begin to see yourself more as you *really* are. The Bible is the only clear glass of truth, the pure silver of love. And it's all waiting there, in front of you, to be discovered.

Drawing from the Well of Prayer

Lord, as I sit at my makeup mirror, help me see the subtle yet significant ways you are turning me into your kind of beautiful woman. Shine through my eyes, Jesus. Pour out my pores. Let your joy lift my lips into a hundred-watt smile. Then show me how to become transparent enough to reflect your image to a world that's searching for all that you are.

Part Three

SPIRIT

Betty Robison

Betty Robison cohosts the
LIFE TODAY television show
with her husband, James.
She is the mother of three children
and the grandmother of eleven.
She and James have been
married for forty years
and live in the
Dallas–Fort Worth area.

The Crushing and Building of My Spirit

My husband, James, has often described our younger daughter, Robin, as "high energy," "strong spirited," and "determined to the end." Robin is now a wife and a mother of three, and we are still amazed at her creative drive to organize her family and household so as to live in the fullness of God's plan.

When Robin was eleven years old, she taught us all an incredible lesson of faith. An unsightly tumor began to grow on the left side of her bottom lip. James and I were immediately concerned and had our family doctor examine it. He felt it wasn't dangerous but encouraged us to have a specialist remove it. I was so disappointed when the specialist told us that he wouldn't be able to schedule the procedure for weeks. But after we left the doctor's office, Robin decided that the delay was a sign that God was going to heal her miraculously.

Extended family and close friends were encouraged by Robin's faith and joined us in praying for healing. I, too, had studied God's Word and believed that he still healed people supernaturally. I prayed day and night for Robin's healing, but as the weeks went by, my faith began to falter. Every time I looked at that grotesque tumor on my beautiful daughter's lip, my heart ached. Robin, however, went through her days as if the tumor didn't exist. Her faith was incredible! I didn't want to discourage her, so when I was having a "low moment," I would go off to my closet, shut the door, and cry out to God in desperation.

Robin's school had scheduled a special program, and she had a significant part to perform. She was confident that the tumor would be gone by then. But when it was still there the week before the school program, I began putting intense pressure on God to

BETTY ROBISON

"do something!" because I couldn't stand it any longer. As my restlessness gave way to sleep, I found myself in the midst of a dream in which I saw Robin coming into our bedroom, holding the tumor in her hand. The dream was so real that I perceived it to be a word from God.

The next morning I eagerly rushed into Robin's room, hoping to see that the tumor was gone. It wasn't. I was heartbroken, but I still shared my dream with Robin. Her excitement about my dream moved her to an even higher level of faith. Later that day as I walked past her bedroom door, I heard Robin talking aloud.

"Honey, who are you talking to?" I called through the door.

Robin popped her head out the door and answered, "I'm practicing my testimony so I'll know just what to say when God heals me."

I smiled bravely and made a quick exit to my room so she wouldn't see me cry.

A few days later as James was preparing to leave town for a meeting, he said, "Betty, I feel that God wants us to pray a very specific prayer about that tumor. I think Robin and I need to trust God to heal her by this Friday." That was only a few days away. I admired Robin and James's big step of faith, and I begged God to come through for my daughter.

On Friday morning Robin awoke to find her hand slapping her bottom lip where the tumor was. When she opened her eyes, she saw what she perceived to be an angel, kneeling by her bed. Then she saw something lying on the sheets. It was the tumor. She quickly looked into the mirror and saw only a tiny red spot on her lip where the tumor had been. She ran into my room shouting, "Mom, it's gone! It's gone!" as she showed me the tumor lying in her hand.

Robin was healed just in time for the school program, and she testified before the whole school about her special miracle from God.

Words of Life

Anyone who becomes as humble as this little child is the greatest in the Kingdom of Heaven. And anyone who welcomes a little child like this on my behalf is welcoming me. *Matthew 18:4-5* Some children were brought to Jesus so he could lay his hands on them and pray for them. The disciples told them not to bother him. But Jesus said, "Let the children come to me. Don't stop them! For the Kingdom of Heaven belongs to such as these." *Matthew 19:13-14*

Living It Out

When you're faced with a difficult or seemingly impossible situation, remind yourself of the faith of a child. Children trust their parents to make the best choices on their behalf. In the same way, God's intervention, whether through supernatural or natural means, is always in our best interest. Make a decision today to fill your heart with faith that he will come through—one way or another, one day or another.

Drawing from the Well of Prayer

Dear Lord, thank you for your Word and your Spirit that grow us in faith and in the understanding of the greatness of your power. Help me to trust and obey you as you carry me through dark and difficult paths. Let my spirit soar to high places with you. Comfort me with your nearness, and speak tender words of love in my ears.

Patsy Clairmont

Patsy Clairmont, the author of such best-selling books as *God Uses Cracked Pots*, *Sportin' a 'Tude*, and *Normal Is Just a Setting on Your Dryer*, is a popular speaker at Women of Faith conferences. She and her husband, Les, have two grown sons and live in Michigan and California.

Playing Hide and Seek with God

How does one find God?

Hmm. Great question, isn't it? God is sort of like the wind: we see evidence of his presence, yet it's not easy to comprehend him. We can't touch him, yet we can feel his presence as surely as we can our own. We don't hear an audible voice, yet at times he speaks as definitely and clearly as anyone we've heard.

I see God's fingerprints in his handiwork: a sunrise, a shooting star, a lilac bush, and a newborn's smile. I observe a measure of his strength in a hurricane, an earthquake, a thunderbolt. I see his creativity in a kangaroo, the Grand Canyon, and a blue-eyed, red-headed baby. I detect his humor in a porpoise, a cactus, and a two-year-old's twinkling eyes. I am aware of his mysteriousness when I consider the Trinity, the solar system, and his desire to be in communion with us: "What are mortals that you should think of us, mere humans that you should care for us?" (Psalm 8:4).

But how do we find God? Sometimes we search him out, and sometimes he "finds" us. Every time we think of God, it is because he first had us on his mind. The Lord is always the initiator. He has been from the beginning (see Genesis 1:1), and he will be to the end (see Revelation 1:7). So know that once you have invited him to enter your life, you are on his mind, and he is in your heart.

That the Lord chooses to settle into our hearts is another mystery. How could we, with our tiny hearts—not to mention our itsy-bitsy brains—house the One who is without beginning or end (see Revelation 1:8)? We could not, aside from his miraculous power and his desire to inhabit us.

I've learned that sometimes we'll be aware of his closeness and sometimes we won't. At times we experience the sweetness of God's nearness and at other times the frightening loneliness of his distance. The Lord hasn't changed locations, but we might have become caught up in our own agendas and forgotten his presence and availability. Other times the Lord will be silently still (scary) for holy purposes (awesome) we don't understand (frustrating), yet . . . (hallelujah!).

How does one find God? Perhaps we need to rest from our pursuit of the Almighty and ask him to reveal himself to us. This is not to say we should stop any honorable efforts to find him, such as attending church regularly, studying the Bible, or enjoying fellowship with other Christians. On the contrary, these endeavors shore us up while we wait. But we must remember that we cannot *command* the Lord into our awareness. He is King; we are his beloved subjects. When our hearts are tenderly responsive ("Whatever, Lord") and it suits the Lord's greater plan, he will lift the thin veil that separates us. And we'll be stunned to realize that he's been closer than our own breath all along.

He's in our prayers guiding our words, in our songs as we worship him; he is filling our mouths when we comfort a friend or speak wisdom to someone who needs hope. Sometimes we can search so hard for the miraculous that we miss the obvious reality of his ever-present nearness. So count your blessings. God is in them, too!

WORDS OF LIFE

Happy are those who hear the joyful call to worship, for they will walk in the light of your presence, Lord. They rejoice all day long in your wonderful reputation. They exult in your righteousness. *Psalm 89:15-16* 🌸 Those who live in the shelter of the Most High will find rest in the shadow of the Almighty. This I declare of the Lord: He alone is my refuge, my place of safety; he is my God, and I am trusting him. *Psalm 91:1-2*

Living It Out

When you feel that God is far from you, find a quiet place. Clear your mind of any daily priorities and agendas or other distractions, and concentrate on opening your heart to God. Listen carefully for that still small voice. It may help to read a favorite psalm or do a Scripture search in an index. Look up words such as *faithful, love, hope, promise*, and then read the listed verses. They will help you focus your thoughts on God, his majesty, and his deep love for you. Ask God to be real to you and to give you a greater awareness of his abiding presence with you.

Drawing from the Well of Prayer

Lord who fills the universe and longs to fill me, please enter my life with your fullness. I long to experience your closeness, but I also will not shun your silence, for you are faithfully continuing your work in both ways. May I be faithful in return, and may my prayer to you always be "Whatever, Lord." Amen.

PATSY CLAIRMONT

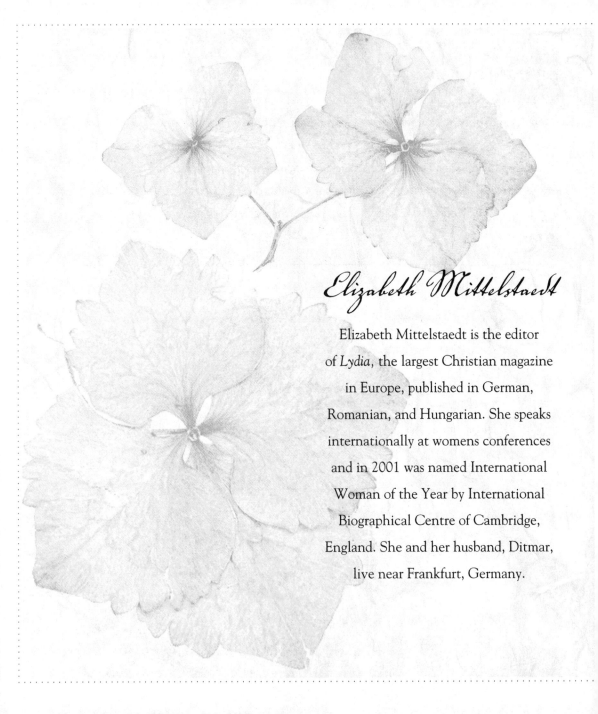

Elizabeth Mittelstaedt

Elizabeth Mittelstaedt is the editor
of *Lydia,* the largest Christian magazine
in Europe, published in German,
Romanian, and Hungarian. She speaks
internationally at womens conferences
and in 2001 was named International
Woman of the Year by International
Biographical Centre of Cambridge,
England. She and her husband, Ditmar,
live near Frankfurt, Germany.

The Comparison Trap

A friend called recently to tell me about a mutual acquaintance who has a new home, an expensive car, and, it seems, the perfect family. The friend who phoned me lives in a small house, drives an old car, and has a child who is in trouble. In her voice I could hear her sadness and disappointment with life.

After listening for a while, I told her about another conversation I'd just had with a woman whose husband had been killed in the prime of life, leaving her alone with two small children.

"You know," I gently reminded my friend on the phone, "it really depends on who we compare ourselves to."

That sentence really jolted my friend out of her self-pity and envy. It helped her realize her life wasn't that bad after all.

I, too, have compared myself with others. For years I struggled over my inability to have a child. Whenever I'd see other women with young children, I'd long for a baby and tell myself, *I'll get pregnant* next *month*. I waited and waited for God to come through, but when nothing—not even adoption—seemed to work out for us, eventually I became angry with God over what I didn't have. I was afraid to admit my anger at God to anyone, including myself.

Then one day it struck me that my life was passing by—and I wasn't living. I finally realized I had to tell God how I felt. I sobbed and sobbed, telling him I loved him and how sorry I was for being angry with him.

About the same time I read a good antidote to the comparison trap of envy: compassion.

ELIZABETH MITTELSTAEDT

"Envy stares at someone else and thinks, 'I wish I had what you have.' Compassion gazes at other people and asks, 'What do I have that I can give to you?' Envy dwells on 'Poor me.' Compassion focuses on 'Poor them.' Envy destroys me, paralyzes me. Compassion rebuilds me, energizes me. Envy is a deadly sin; compassion, a wonderful, Christlike virtue." I knew then that I needed to focus not on what I *didn't* have but what I *did* have.

Do you envy someone who's taller, slimmer, or younger? Do you wish you had a better paying job, a husband, or a more wonderful husband? Do you compare yourself with someone who lives in a beautiful house, has perfect children, and a doctoral degree?

I've found that thanking God for his gifts helps me focus on his blessings in my life that I can so easily take for granted—food to eat, a warm bed to sleep in, and family and friends who love me.

What are you thankful for today? As you consciously fill your mind with the good things God has given you, there will be no more room for envy!

Words of Life

[Jesus said,] "Look at the lilies and how they grow. They don't work or make their clothing, yet Solomon in all his glory was not dressed as beautifully as they are. And if God cares so wonderfully for flowers that are here today and gone tomorrow, won't he more surely care for you?" *Luke 12:27-28* Love is patient and kind. Love is not jealous or boastful or proud or rude. *1 Corinthians 13:4-5* Give all your worries and cares to God, for he cares about what happens to you. *1 Peter 5:7*

Living It Out

Are you feeling discouraged about what others have and you don't? Then make a list of all the blessings, large and small, that God has granted you. Have you just found a job that you love after years of feeling trapped at a job you detested? Maybe you don't like your small apartment, but it's close to a forest preserve and you love to hike. Instead of envying what others have, make a habit of focusing on the good things God has given you.

Drawing from the Well of Prayer

Lord Jesus, thank you for creating me, just as I am, and for showering me with blessings every day. Help me see those blessings as gifts from a God who loves me always. Keep me from focusing on what others have. Remind me to keep my eyes on you instead of on the things of this world. And help me to learn contentment.

Jeanne Rogers

Jeanne Rogers has worked
with James and Betty Robison
in music ministry for more
than thirty years. She has
produced a number of worship
cassettes and CDs and is also
a writer. Jeanne and her husband,
Jim, executive vice-president
of LIFE Outreach,
have three children.

No Substitute for God's Plan

Over a five-year span I had received many personal promises from the Lord preparing me to be a worship leader. Music was my passion, and I was excited—and a bit scared—as I prepared to enter a new season of ministry. But on my very first opportunity to lead worship, I learned a difficult lesson.

The small conference would take me to another state, far from my familiar and supportive surroundings. For twenty years I had been a featured soloist for James Robison's large crusades across the U.S. and had never experienced any fear in that role. However, this particular conference would be hosting men and women from a more conservative denomination, and I was concerned about how they would respond to a more intimate style of worship than what they were accustomed to. God had been assuring me with glorious promises and visions of the good things that would happen if I obeyed his call to use my voice for him. But now that the opportunity had finally arrived, I was terrified!

I'd been told that I could bring whatever keyboard player I wanted, so I called Kirk Dearman, a well-known worship leader and songwriter. He agreed to play, sing, and even bring his talented wife, Debbie, to sing and assist me in my first experience of leading worship.

We planned our music, rehearsed, and traveled together to the conference. Kirk had no idea I was so afraid. Secretly I planned to let him take the lead in the first service. I thought if I felt confident, I might step into the leadership role later in the week. But God's "perfect plan" began to unfold early the first morning of the conference.

"Jeanne?" The voice on the phone sounded worried.

"Yes."

"This is Debbie. Kirk is really sick this morning."

"What's wrong?"

"His temperature is 105 degrees, and he's lost his voice."

As I hung up the phone, I felt as if God were shaking his finger in my face as if to say, *You thought you could slip this one by me, didn't you? Now I have taken away your substitutes and your crutches. You'll have to trust me.*

He was right; I was cornered. Now I'd have to lead worship by myself—and worse, without any instruments! I fell to my knees and asked God to give me the faith to lead his people to encounter him.

That morning I stepped onto the platform of the church, and God poured down his anointing in a way I haven't experienced since. At one point we knelt in worship, afraid to move or speak. We were being held—suspended under the weight of God's glory. An incredibly long and peaceful silence filled the room, and we just basked in the presence of God.

I've been in some very powerful services since that time, but I've never led a service that could compare to that first desperate experience. Such a humble beginning launched me into my destiny. I didn't know it at the time, but later I would stand before a gathering of ten thousand believers in my next conference at James Robison's Bible conference in Dallas. Many large conferences would follow over a period of ten years.

God was merciful in teaching me up front to stop looking for a substitute and simply obey him. If we trust him to equip us, we'll be able to walk the path that he has charted. And when we follow his plan, he gives us precious promises and the power of the Holy Spirit to guide us.

WORDS OF LIFE

Trust in the Lord with all your heart; do not depend on your own understanding. Seek his will in all you do, and he will direct your paths. Don't be impressed with your own wisdom.

Instead, fear the Lord and turn your back on evil. *Proverbs 3:5-7* "My thoughts are completely different from yours," says the Lord. "And my ways are far beyond anything you could imagine. For just as the heavens are higher than the earth, so are my ways higher than your ways and my thoughts higher than your thoughts." *Isaiah 55:8-9* Don't copy the behavior and customs of this world, but let God transform you into a new person by changing the way you think. Then you will know what God wants you to do, and you will know how good and pleasing and perfect his will really is. *Romans 12:2*

LIVING IT OUT

Think about the plans God may have for your life and ministry. Are you ready and willing to follow God's lead, or are you staying in the background, looking for a substitute to take your place? Make a point to do at least one thing this week that will bring you closer to fulfilling God's perfect plan for the gifts he's given you to use in blessing others.

Drawing from the Well of Prayer

Lord, I submit my life to you, a living sacrifice. Renew my mind and transform it from the world's way of thinking so I might understand your perfect will for my life. Lead me by your Holy Spirit. Fill me with the knowledge of your plan, and give me strength and wisdom to make choices that will prepare and equip me for your call.

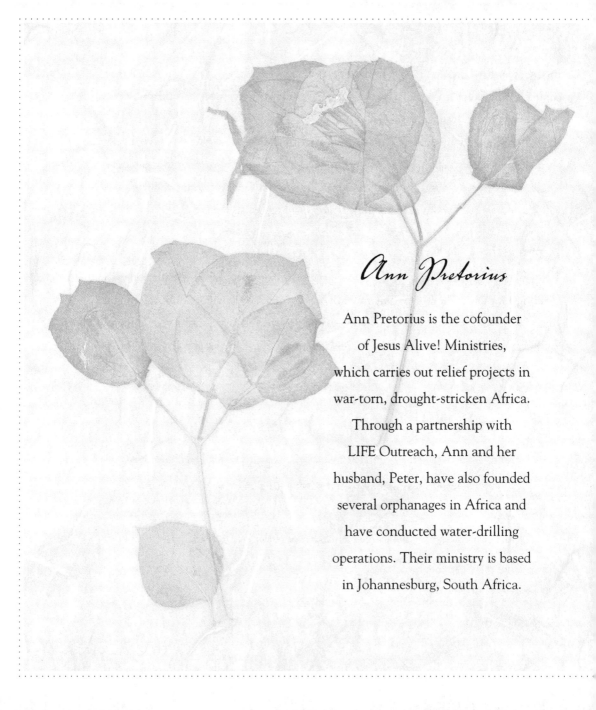

Ann Pretorius

Ann Pretorius is the cofounder
of Jesus Alive! Ministries,
which carries out relief projects in
war-torn, drought-stricken Africa.
Through a partnership with
LIFE Outreach, Ann and her
husband, Peter, have also founded
several orphanages in Africa and
have conducted water-drilling
operations. Their ministry is based
in Johannesburg, South Africa.

Forgiving Grace

Early one morning the telephone rang. It was my older sister, and she had devastating news to share. Our youngest sister, Terri, and her husband, Jay, had been murdered in South Africa, and their four-year-old son and twenty-one-month-old daughter were now orphans. The murderer was the man who had become known as the "Hammerman." He had broken into the homes of several victims and brutally beaten them to death with a hammer.

To make matters worse, if that were possible, Terri and Jay died at the hands of a black South African. I had heard of such tragedies occurring in South Africa and often wondered how I would react if I ever faced such a cruel circumstance. I had prayed that our ministry to the black African people would shield us from such evil.

As my sister's shocking message replayed in my head, I began to cry out to God. Instantly I felt God's power come upon me, and I had a strong urge to pray: "Father, forgive him; he did not know what he was doing." As those words came out of my mouth, I became aware of a river of forgiveness flowing out of my spirit.

Feelings of hatred, anger, and unforgiveness toward this man, who had taken the precious lives of my loved ones, threatened to overtake my emotions, but the strength of the river would not let these feelings take root. The flow of God's forgiving grace was obliterating them.

My initial experience with God's forgiving grace was with my own sin. I had asked him to forgive me in a prayer of salvation, and he extended his mercy to me. I had memorized the Lord's Prayer and understood that I must forgive others' trespasses against me as I am forgiven my trespasses. But when faced with this seemingly impossible task of forgiving the man who killed my family members, my greatest inspiration came from Jesus himself. He extended mercy to cruel, godless men even as he was dying from the terrible wounds those men had inflicted on him.

Another source of inspiration for me was realizing that the Father sacrificed his own Son to offer forgiveness to a degraded, dying world—and to sinners like me. He knew that once our hearts were open to receive it, his unfathomable grace could empower us to face any crisis in life.

I could so easily have become embittered toward the native South African people after what happened to my sister's family. I could have abandoned the evangelistic and humanitarian relief work that my husband and I had begun. But God worked a supernatural healing within me. I forgave and let God's indescribable comfort absorb the shock and pain of losing Terri and Jay.

Instead of "returning evil for evil," my husband and I increased our work of "blessing." Today our ministry, Jesus Alive! reaches millions of people in twelve countries within sub-Saharan Africa. We take food, water, clothing, and medical supplies to these impoverished and war-torn countries. We establish agriculture projects, dig water wells, and build schools. But, most of all, we take the transforming message of God's love and forgiveness.

Words of Life

Dear friends, never avenge yourselves. Leave that to God. For it is written, "I will take vengeance; I will repay those who deserve it," says the Lord. Instead, do what the Scriptures say: "If your enemies are hungry, feed them. If they are thirsty, give them something to drink, and they will be ashamed of what they have done to you." Don't let evil get the best of you, but conquer evil by doing good. *Romans 12:19-21* Get rid of all bitterness, rage, anger, harsh words, and slander, as well as all types of malicious behavior. Instead, be kind to each other, tenderhearted, forgiving one another, just as God through Christ has forgiven you. Follow God's example in everything you do, because you are his dear children. *Ephesians 4:31–5:1* All of you should be of one mind, full of sympathy toward each other, loving one another with tender hearts and humble minds. Don't repay evil for evil. Don't retaliate when people say unkind things about you. Instead, pay them back with a blessing. That is what God wants you to do, and he will bless you for it. *1 Peter 3:8-9*

LIVING IT OUT

If you are facing a dark situation or season and your emotions threaten to overtake you, realize that there is a river of God's grace that flows down to you. Cry out to your heavenly Father, believing that he will supply whatever is needed to sustain you. God has enough love and grace to surround you and hold you. He has a plan to comfort and strengthen you. He wants you to know him intimately. You cannot do this in your own strength, but God has the power—and he desires to give it to you.

Drawing from the Well of Prayer

Father, empower me to forgive others as freely as you have forgiven me. I recognize I can't do this on my own. You'll have to do it through me by the power of your Holy Spirit. I open myself to you. Come and fill me with your love and grace.

CeCe Winans

CeCe Winans's musical fame speaks for itself. In 1995 she released her first solo album, *Alone in His Presence*, after producing five albums with brother BeBe—*BeBe & CeCe Winans*, *Heaven*, *Different Lifestyles*, *First Christmas*, and *Relationships* (all Sparrow/Capitol)— all of which have sold millions in both mainstream and gospel markets and garnered over seven Grammy awards, seven Gospel Music Association Awards, five Stellar Awards, three NAACP Image Awards, and a Soul Train Music Award. But despite such an impressive array of accomplishments and numerous television appearances, CeCe prefers her role as wife and mother to that of performer.

Fully Surrendered

I didn't plan a career as a singer. In fact, although I grew up with parents who were gospel singers, the idea of being on stage by myself was not only far from my mind, it was in the category of impossible. I was about the shyest child you could imagine. Even today I'm amazed that I'm singing in front of *anybody*, much less a large audience. Although I've had to outgrow some of my shyness just because of what God has called me to do, I still get nervous. I'd much rather be at home in my own kitchen than up on the stage. When someone asks me to sing, I'm great at making excuses. But my husband, Alvin, who believes in me more than I do in myself, smiles and says, "Would you be quiet and just do what God wants you to do?"

It's a lesson I should have learned a long time ago, and yet I'm still learning it: *If God calls you to do something, he'll equip you to do it.* It sounds like an easy phrase, but it's a tough one to live out. When I look at myself, I tend to think, *I don't have what it takes. I'm not this. I'm not that. And that person over there could certainly do it better.*

But God doesn't always ask us to do what's easy. He knows all of us have bad days and good days. And thank God we do, for our very imperfection showcases how much we need God on a daily basis. God delights in using people who don't feel adequate . . . or talented . . . or special. Why? Because then we know beyond a shadow of a doubt that he's the one who accomplished what we thought was impossible. We didn't do it—*he* did! And then he gets the praise.

So many times we want God's blessings, but we shy away from the process it takes to get them. We want God to be faithful, but we don't want to be faithful ourselves. There's so much God wants to do for us—inside, in our own spirits—but many times we're not ready for him. God wants a relationship with us, but he patiently waits for us to allow him fully into our lives. Perhaps that's why the hymn "I Surrender All" has become my favorite, because that's what I constantly try to do—turn everything over to God. That means my priorities, my impossible-to-accomplish "to do" list, my problem relationship, my sometimes exhaustion. It means holding nothing back from the One who knows us so intimately anyway. And when we do that—surrender our spirits entirely to our almighty Father— something miraculous happens. Our problems suddenly seem so small because God is so great. Our spirits soar, and we are able to do things we could never imagine doing on our own power.

Words of Life

Be strong and courageous! Do not be afraid or discouraged. For the Lord your God is with you wherever you go. *Joshua 1:9* 　Those who wait on the Lord will find new strength. They will fly high on wings like eagles. They will run and not grow weary. They will walk and not faint. *Isaiah 40:31* 　[Jesus said,] "I have told you all this so that you may have peace in me. Here on earth you will have many trials and sorrows. But take heart, because I have overcome the world." *John 16:33*

Living it Out

If you want to have God's blessings in your life and his hand on your spirit, follow this key principle every day: Put God first. If you live out this principle daily in your work, your personal life, and your relationships, then everything else will fall in line. This doesn't mean life will always be easy, but you'll know you are doing what's right. And as you put him first, Jesus will become more precious to you than you have ever known before!

Drawing from the Well of Prayer

Lord, it's not always easy putting you first. And it is easy to let my daily agenda distract me from what you most want me to do. Help me to be open to your Spirit's leading in every area of my life. And, like Mary, who sat at your feet, help me remember what's most important—learning what you want me to do and then doing it.

❧ ❧ ❧

Terry Dorian, Ph.D.

Terry Dorian, a health researcher
for more than twenty years, is an expert
in the use of whole foods for the
prevention and cure of degenerative
disease. Dr. Dorian has written several
books and is a popular speaker and
radio and television personality.

Accepting God's Plan

As children of God we know that he has a purpose and a plan for every circumstance in our lives. And we also know he uses all of the happy and unhappy events in our lives to conform us to his image (see Romans 8:28-29). But it takes time to learn this rock-bottom truth of our faith, and I didn't know the truth of Romans 8:29 until my first husband died.

During that stressful time my prayers became arguments with God. I could not—I would not—accept my circumstances. The finality of death tormented me. I could do nothing, absolutely nothing, to alter the finality of death. However, I eventually submitted to God's Word. One day in May of 1978, not quite two months after Frank died, I read Romans chapter 8 as though for the first time. I saw the truth; I believed it; I realized that God loved Frank and God loved me! I would come to love his plan.

Since then I've learned that confessing, repenting, and receiving God's grace and mercy are the basis of every victory we enjoy in Christ, and that is certainly true of victory over stress. The Word cleanses us as the Holy Spirit prepares our hearts.

The Lord himself tells us in John 15:3 that we are clean because of the Word that he has spoken to us: "You have already been pruned for greater fruitfulness by the message I have given you." The faith that brings forth our redemption comes into our hearts by the power of his Word. As Romans 10:17 says, "Faith comes from listening to this message of good news—the Good News about Christ."

Many stress-management writers, even those who are Christians, tell us to "manage stress" by making sure we have proper rest and diversions. They suggest making time for

TERRY DORIAN, PH.D.

recreation, such as hobbies and sports activities. But that advice works only for those who have the financial freedom to deliver themselves from all that is stressful.

What about people in other cultures whose idea of a good day is being able to find enough food to stay alive? And what about the families in this country who are working long hours or several jobs, just to make enough money for essentials? Praise God that although we may have little or no money for diversions, we can have his peace. God's Word is for the rich and the poor. His answers don't depend on our being able to circumvent our circumstances.

Seeking distractions from our "stress" is very different from exulting in our tribulations. The goal of the rest, relaxation, and diversion strategies is comfort. But tribulation has another purpose—building character. The tennis court, an evening out, a vacation, may be useful for some aspects of our lives, but they aren't useful as a means of enabling us to bear our problems. Is God unfair to those who cannot afford to divert themselves with pleasantries? No. He will enable us to exult in our tribulation. Our circumstances have meaning. They are part of his plan. If we trust the Planner, we can trust the plan.

Stress-management techniques will help us to feel better, work better, accomplish more. But we must be sure that we incorporate those techniques into the real business of our lives—allowing God's Word to come alive in our hearts and produce the fruit that he desires from us.

WORDS OF LIFE

You have turned my mourning into joyful dancing. You have taken away my clothes of mourning and clothed me with joy. *Psalm 30:11* What I want . . . is your true thanks to God; I want you to fulfill your vows to the Most High. Trust me in your times of trouble, and I will rescue you, and you will give me glory. *Psalm 50:14-15* I have learned how to get along happily whether I have much or little. I know how to live on almost nothing or with everything. I have learned the secret of living in every situation, whether it is with a full stomach or empty, with plenty or little. For I can do everything with the help of Christ who gives me the strength I need. *Philippians 4:11-13*

LIVING IT OUT

The importance of stressful circumstances is that they allow us to discover who we are. Remind yourself that only through the circumstances of life do we recognize our sinful nature. Recognizing our failures can be liberating! Remember, too, that fear and unbelief cause us to deny our sin, but when we repent and confess our sins to God, we find ourselves safely in his arms.

Drawing from the Well of Prayer

Lord Jesus, help me to embrace my circumstances as from you. I confess and repent of any sin and of not trusting your sovereignty and goodness. I offer you my sacrifice of thanksgiving. I will sing praise and shout for joy, even in the middle of tribulation. For then I will be renewed in the spirit of my mind to receive every blessing that you have for me through life's trials and tribulations.

TERRY DORIAN, PH.D.

Nancie Carmichael

Nancie Carmichael was copublisher
of *Virtue* magazine with her husband,
Bill, for eleven years, editor for two
years, and then editor-at-large.
She is the coauthor of *Lord, Bless My
Child* and *Lord, Bless This Marriage*,
and the author of *Your Life, God's Home*
and *The Deeper Life*. In recognition of
her rich and varied ministry to women,
Nancie received an honorary doctoral
degree from Western Baptist College.
Nancie and Bill have five children and
live in Black Butte Ranch, Oregon.

Mountaintop Experiences

A beautiful meadow lies near the summit of a rugged mountain not far from my home. When friends told my husband, Bill, and me that the hike was well worth the trek, we and three of our children started out. As we marched single file through a tunnel of trees, the path seemed to go nowhere. It wound up and around for miles through tall stands of trees. Several times we found ourselves at a fork in the path, and we wondered which of the paths that angled out was the main one. As we trudged upward, we weren't always sure we had stayed on the right course. The path itself was rocky, tedious, and dangerous.

When the kids grumbled about their aching legs or one of us nearly twisted an ankle, I began to wonder whether the effort was worth it. Then the fragrance of wildflowers filled the air. *How could this be?* I thought. *It's dark here. The sunlight is screened by dense trees.* But soon the path widened, and there it was: a beautiful, sun-drenched meadow fed by streams that cascaded from a glacier clinging to the side of the mountain. We caught our breath. It was too lovely to imagine.

The meadow was a mass of wildflowers of every variety and growing so thickly that it reminded me of an enormous English garden. Enchanted, we took off our shoes and sat by the stream. *Surely this must be like heaven,* we thought. We ate our lunch, savoring our surroundings. All too soon it was time to go back.

As we made our way down the mountain, I thought of Jesus and his disciples on the Mount of Transfiguration, when God's glory came and Moses and Elijah spoke with Jesus (see Luke 9:28-36). I can identify with Peter, who, after this glorious mountaintop experience with the Lord, suggested, "Master, this is wonderful! We will make three shrines—

one for you, one for Moses, and one for Elijah." In other words, "Let's build a temple here so that we can come here often and make this experience last forever!"

Like Peter, I would like to "enshrine" the mountaintop experiences, to capture those rare places of victory when I sense God's presence and his pleasure in me.

But to be honest, those times are rare. Many more times are like the climb up the mountain—exhausting, uncertain, painful, tedious. Bill and I have rocky times. Sometimes mothering is very hard work. Some days the ministry God has called me to feels as if it isn't going anywhere.

But the longer I live, the more convinced I am that the struggle—the journey itself— is significant, necessary. Jesus "was willing to die a shameful death on the cross because of the joy he knew would be his afterward" (Hebrews 12:2). Endurance is a difficult path, and often it's lonely. And yet, to get to the beautiful places, you must endure.

Perhaps there's something in your life now that's a struggle for you and you're tempted to give up. Many voices today would tell you that nobody should have to work this hard, that nothing is worth this kind of pain. But the battle is won not so much in blinding moments of truth as in hanging in there when the going is tough. Don't give up. If you are following the Lord, the path will lead to a beautiful place. So keep climbing. It will be worth it.

WORDS OF LIFE

Your word is a lamp for my feet and a light for my path. *Psalm 119:105* 🌿 Do not throw away this confident trust in the Lord, no matter what happens. Remember the great reward it brings you! Patient endurance is what you need now, so you will continue to do God's will. Then you will receive all that he has promised. *Hebrews 10:35-36*

LIVING IT OUT

Remember always that there are songs yet to be sung. Paintings yet to be created. Books yet to be written. Lives to be touched for God. Families to be forged. Marriages to be crafted. Lives of integrity to be lived. For you to accomplish these things, you must persevere, staying on the path and allowing God's Word to light your way.

Drawing from the Well of Prayer

God, our life paths sometimes seem dark. Help us to open our eyes to you in the midst of those struggles. If we do so, we know that the fragrance of your presence will linger with us and will urge us to stay the course so we can receive all you have promised.

Luci Swindoll

After an early retirement from
a career with a major oil company,
Luci became vice president of public
relations at Insight for Living,
her brother Chuck Swindoll's
international radio ministry. From
there she "retired" to fulfill an
ambitious speaking schedule,
traveling across the United States,
motivating and inspiring her
audiences. She has written numerous
books, including *Celebrating Life*,
and is also a main speaker for the
Women of Faith conferences.

Seize the Day!

It's a funny thing about time: Every one of us knows we have only twenty-four hours a day, yet we try our best to think of ways to make each day last longer or become shorter to suit our preferences. While the clock ticks out the same number of minutes at the same rate every day, we try to *save* them like pennies in a jar, so we can *spend* them someday somewhere else, whenever we choose.

That's not a bad idea, but it just doesn't work that way. Many of us cannot grasp the truth that the time allotted to us on this earth is sufficient for all the Lord has planned for us to do. We don't need one minute more or one minute less to accomplish the job: the job of living.

When I was a child, our family had a chiming clock that had been handed down through the generations and was a well-loved treasure. On the hour, of course, it chimed out the time, and by it we kept on schedule with meals and departures and awakening and sleeping. Often from our respective bedrooms each of us called out the number of chimes until the last one stopped.

One night after we had all gone to bed about midnight, the clock began to chime, and we started our audible ritual: "Nine . . . ten . . . eleven . . . twelve." Just as we closed our mouths after shouting out, "TWELVE!" the clock struck thirteen. We could hardly believe our ears. *Where did that come from?* I wondered, as we all laughed heartily from our beds. Then, almost in perfect unison, we called out, "It's later than you think!"

For most of us, that's the problem: our greatest fear is running out of time. So we hurry through life trying desperately to get everything done: working overtime, eating fast food in the car, racing down the freeway. Life itself encourages us to hurry. I can do my laundry twice as fast as my grandmother did; I can travel coast to coast faster than my father ever could; with a few keystrokes and clicks of the mouse I can handle correspondence that took my mother hours. Yet I seem to have less time than they did. What has happened?

In our quest to save time we're losing something. My grandparents, for example, always had time for my parents and my brothers and me; they had time for music in their home; they emphasized beautifully served meals, family reunions, and long conversations. It seemed they had time for everything in life that was important because they took time to live. They treasured the biblical injunction that proclaims, "This is the day the Lord has made. We will rejoice and be glad in it" (Psalm 118:24).

What about you? Do you seize each day with passionate vigor?

Don't wait for some other time. Tonight your clock could strike thirteen. It's later than you think, so rejoice in this day and be glad!

Words of Life

There is a time for everything, a season for every activity under heaven. . . . People should eat and drink and enjoy the fruits of their labor, for these are gifts from God. *Ecclesiastes 3:1, 13* 🦋 Don't worry about tomorrow, for tomorrow will bring its own worries. Today's trouble is enough for today. *Matthew 6:34* 🦋 The time that remains is very short. . . . This world and all it contains will pass away. *1 Corinthians 7:29-31*

Living It Out

Think of something that takes a bit of extra time to do—and then *do* it. Do it for yourself. Do it for a family member. Do it for a neighbor or friend. Do it for the Lord. Maybe it will be an act of generosity or a moment of kindness directed toward a loved one or a stranger.

Perhaps it will be simply singing a hymn of praise and thanksgiving because your heart is full of gratitude. Whatever it is, take the time to do it—and rejoice in the day the Lord has given you!

Drawing from the Well of Prayer

Father, give me the grace today to take time. Time to be with you. Time to be with others. Time to enjoy the life you have given me. Help me to remember that today is the day you have made. May I rejoice and be glad in it! Amen.

Carole Mayhall

Carole Mayhall is the author
of numerous books, including
Come Walk with Me and
Help, Lord, I'm Sinking:
Lessons from My Rocking Boat.
She and her husband, Jack,
live in Colorado Springs.

The Secret to Joy

I know that a heart occupied with God is a joy-filled heart. Yet I admit I often have days (weeks? months?) when I'm discouraged or disgruntled. The reason isn't that I don't understand the big picture. I can see clearly the mountains of God's faithfulness, sovereignty, and incredible love. But my joy is often ruined by small blotches on the canvas.

I discovered one such mar early in my walk with God. Soon after my husband, Jack, and I were married, the owner of the home we moved into informed us he'd decided to turn the efficiency apartments surrounding our house into a motel, and he asked Jack and me to be the rental agents for it. That meant someone needed to be at home twenty-four hours a day—and most of the time I was that someone. Soon the person who cleaned the units quit, and I found myself not only "managing" the motel but cleaning the rooms.

Scrubbing one of the motel toilets one day, I grumbled to the Lord. "You know, Lord," I said, "I could be leading a Bible study. I could be talking to the neighbors about Christ. I could be taking a meal to a shut-in. I could be doing lots of things that would be more useful and certainly more pleasant!"

And there, sitting on the floor and scrubbing that toilet, I heard him speak to my heart: *Carole, whatever you do, do it heartily for me.*

"Even cleaning motel toilets, Lord?"

Even cleaning motel toilets, Child.

It dawned on me that I could scrub floors, cook meals, dust, chauffeur people, serve in a multitude of ways, and serve God heartily in doing so. If that was how he wanted me to spend my time, well, that was his business. I could do it for God! Knowing that made all the difference in my attitude.

I have an inkling that this is one lesson God will continue reminding me of the rest of my life. If I'm not learning (and relearning) it, the "dailies" of life—those miserable, mundane jobs, those dirty, no-one-else-will-do-them tasks—become not just drudgery but downright depressing, and joy will disappear.

But when stressful situations and difficult times threaten to bring the scum of my life (a bad attitude) to the surface, it's my choice whether to stir that scum into my everyday circumstances or to maintain a joyful attitude and ask God to skim the scum from my life. Part of living joyfully rests on the decision to endure unpleasant situations as a sacrifice of praise to God.

Author Paul Thigpen defines joy as "the sense of delight that arises within us in the presence of someone or something we love." He goes on to say, "Joy depends not on our acquisition of something, but rather on our encounter with something." That something is Someone—God, who renews us every day. To be more joyful, we need to drink in God's presence. As we spend more time in his Word, he reveals more of what we need for joy. And then we can overflow with joy, no matter what we're doing!

Words of Life

Let your good deeds shine out for all to see, so that everyone will praise your heavenly Father. *Matthew 5:16* 🍃 Work hard and cheerfully at whatever you do, as though you were working for the Lord rather than for people. *Colossians 3:23* 🍃 May the Lord make your love grow and overflow to each other and to everyone else, just as our love overflows toward you. . . . We urge you in the name of the Lord Jesus to live in a way that pleases God, as we have taught you. You are doing this already, and we encourage you to do so more and more. *1 Thessalonians 3:12; 4:1*

LIVING IT OUT

If you were to draw a circle to represent your life, what would be in the center—your problems or God? If your problems are at the center, you will always walk in despair. But if God is at the center, you will walk in joy through your problems, even when you're struggling. Joy is a matter of attitude. So ask yourself, are you doing something because you have no choice, because you hope to please people—or because you want to please God?

Drawing from the Well of Prayer

Lord, I want to live for you. Help me work toward the goal of pleasing you more and myself and others less. In everything I do, let me obey your command to "work hard and cheerfully" so others will see you in me and give you praise.

SOURCES

We gratefully acknowledge the publishers and authors from which some of the included material has been adapted:

Lisa Bevere, *You Are Not What You Weigh* (Orlando, Fla.: Creation House, 1998), 27–35, 43–44, 46, 50, 146–147. Interview on *LIFE TODAY*'s show, *Another View*, 2000.

Bonnie Budzowski, "Loneliness: Can It Be a Gift?" This article first appeared in *Today's Christian Woman* magazine (September/October 1995), published by Christianity Today Int'l., Carol Stream, Illinois.

Patsy Clairmont, *Joy Breaks* (Grand Rapids, Mich.: Zondervan, 1997).

Terry Dorian, *Health Begins in Him* (Lafayette, La.: Huntington House, 1995), 68–73.

Verla Gillmor, "Need a Confidence Boost?" This article first appeared in *Today's Christian Woman* magazine (May/June 2000), published by Christianity Today Int'l., Carol Stream, Illinois.

Liz Curtis Higgs, adapted from "Beautiful to Behold" (12–14) and "Confidentially Speaking" (113–114) in *Rise and Shine: A Devotional* (Nashville: Thomas Nelson, 2002).

Carolyn Johnson, interview on *LIFE TODAY*.

Cathy Lechner, *Couldn't We Just Kill 'Em and Tell God They Died?* (Orlando, Fla.: Creation House, 1997), 52–55.

Carole Mayhall, "The Secret to Joy." This article first appeared in *Today's Christian Woman* magazine (March/April 1998), published by Christianity Today Int'l., Carol Stream, Illinois.

Joy Michaels, "I Was Sexually Abused." This article first appeared in *Today's Christian Woman* magazine (November/December 1999), published by Christianity Today Int'l., Carol Stream, Illinois.

Cheryl K. (Ewings) Miller, "When Depression Hits Home." This article first appeared in *Today's Christian Woman* magazine (November/December 1999), published by Christianity Today Int'l., Carol Stream, Illinois.

Linda Mintle, *Getting Unstuck* (Orlando, Fla.: Creation House Publishers, 1999), 229–270. Interview on *LIFE TODAY*'s show, *Another View*, 2000.

Elizabeth Mittelstaedt, "One Woman's Choice." This article first appeared in *Today's Christian Woman* magazine (May/June 1995), published by Christianity Today Int'l., Carol Stream, Illinois.

Elizabeth Mittelstaedt, "The Comparison Trap." This article first appeared in *Today's Christian Woman* magazine (March/April 1995), published by Christianity Today Int'l., Carol Stream, Illinois.

Beth Moore, "Bitter or Better?" Adapted from "The Lord Who Heals Us," in *Finding God's Peace in Perilous Times* (Wheaton, Ill.: Tyndale, 2001), 37–41. Copyright © 2001 by Beth Moore. All rights reserved. Used by permission.

Elizabeth Newenhuyse, "Cultivating Contentment." This article first appeared in *Today's Christian Woman* magazine (September/October 1994), published by Christianity Today Int'l., Carol Stream, Illinois.

Kathryn S. Olson, "The Empty Crib." This article first appeared in *Today's Christian Woman* magazine (May/June 2000), published by Christianity Today Int'l., Carol Stream, Illinois.

Chonda Pierce, interviews on *LIFE TODAY*.

Ann Pretorius, "Forgiving Grace," first appeared in *Women at the Well: 31 Refreshing Devotions for Every Facet of a Woman's Life*, originally published in 2001 by Life Publishing, Fort Worth, Texas.

Rhonda Redmon, "Living without the Answers," first appeared in *Women at the Well: 31 Refreshing Devotions for Every Facet of a Woman's Life*, originally published in 2001 by Life Publishing, Fort Worth, Texas.

Betty Robison, "The Crushing and Building of My Spirit," "Threefold Fitness," and "Waiting for God's Best," first appeared in *Women at the Well: 31 Refreshing Devotions for Every Facet of a Woman's Life*, originally published in 2001 by Life Publishing, Fort Worth, Texas.

Jeanne Rogers, "No Substitute for God's Plan," first appeared in *Women at the Well: 31 Refreshing Devotions for Every Facet of a Woman's Life*, originally published in 2001 by Life Publishing, Fort Worth, Texas.

Luci Swindoll, *Joy Breaks* (Grand Rapids, Mich.: Zondervan, 1997).

Ramona Cramer Tucker, "One on One with CeCe Winans." This article first appeared in *Today's Christian Woman* magazine (September/October 1995), published by Christianity Today Int'l., Carol Stream, Illinois.

Ramona Cramer Tucker, "Kathy Troccoli's Mission of Love." This article first appeared in *Today's Christian Woman* magazine (March/April 1995), published by Christianity Today Int'l., Carol Stream, Illinois.

Robin Turner, "The Best Job in the World," first appeared in *Women at the Well: 31 Refreshing Devotions for Every Facet of a Woman's Life*, previously published in 2001 by Life Publishing, Fort Worth, Texas.

Lynn Vanderzalm, *Finding Strength in Weakness* (Grand Rapids, Mich.: Zondervan, 1995).

Marcia Van't Land, *Living Well with Chronic Illness* (Wheaton, Ill.: Harold Shaw, 1993).

136